Book of Days

...Living the New Rebellion

Oh, love the LORD, all you His saints!

Psalm 31:23 NKJV

Book of Days

...Living the New Rebellion™

365 Ways to Ignite Your Passion for God
and Supercharge Your Life

NELSON BOOKS
A Division of Thomas Nelson Publishers
Since 1798

www.thomasnelson.com

Copyright © 2006 by GRQ, Inc.

All rights reserved. No portion of this book may be reproduced, stored in a retrieval system, or transmitted in any form or by any means—electronic, mechanical, photocopy, recording, scanning, or other—except for brief quotations in critical reviews or articles, without the prior written permission of the publisher.

Published in Nashville, Tennessee, by Thomas Nelson, Inc.

Nelson Books titles may be purchased in bulk for educational, business, fund-raising, or sales promotional use. For information, please e-mail SpecialMarkets@ThomasNelson.com.

Scripture quotations noted NKJV are from The New King James Version®. Copyright © 1979, 1980, 1982 by Thomas Nelson, Inc. Used by permission. All rights reserved.

Scripture quotations noted MSG are from *The Message*. Copyright © by Eugene H. Peterson 1993, 1994, 1995. Used by permission of NavPress Publishing Group.

Scripture quotations noted NIV are from the Holy Bible: New International Version®. Copyright © 1973, 1978, 1984 by International Bible Society. Used by permission of Zondervan Publishing House. All rights reserved.

Scripture quotations noted NLT are from the *Holy Bible*, New Living Translation, copyright © 1996. Used by permission of Tyndale House Publishers, Inc., Wheaton, Illinois 60189. All rights reserved.

Scripture quotations noted NASB are from the New American Standard Bible®, copyright © 1960, 1962, 1963, 1968, 1971, 1973, 1975, 1977, 1995 by The Lockman Foundation. Used by permission.

Scripture quotations noted HCSB have been taken from the Holman Christian Standard Bible®, Copyright © 1999, 2000, 2002, 2003 by Holman Bible Publishers. Used by permission. Holman Christian Standard Bible®, Holman CSB® and HCSB® are federally registered trademarks of Holman Bible Publishers.

Managing Editor: Lila Empson
Associate Editor: Bryan Norman
Manuscript: Jerome Daley
Design: Whisner Design Group
Creative Direction: Betsy Wilson Mancuso

ISBN 10: 0-7852-1870-X
ISBN 13: 978-0-7852-1870-8

Printed in Canada

08 09 10 9 8 7 6 5 4

Watch, stand fast in the faith, be brave, be strong.
Let all that you do be done with love.

1 Corinthians 16:13–14 NKJV

Contents

book of days

book of days

Introduction

The New Rebellion. What's it all about?

Rebellion occurs when oppression reaches a level that we can no longer tolerate in good conscience. It occurs when our vision for extraordinary living is more compelling than our urge for comfort. Oppression can be subtle. Sometimes we feel it inside our souls, and sometimes we feel it on the outside. Today's world is full of both kinds. Materialism numbs us from the outside while distraction and apathy work on us from the inside. When that happens, it's time to rebel.

The New Rebellion calls to today's emerging generation, to *your* generation. It calls to people who are disillusioned with MTV culture, tired of halfhearted Christianity. The New Rebellion calls to all of us who want to rise above the accepted norms of society and lay hold of a life beyond our wildest dreams. If that describes you, then join the uprising of ordinary men and women who have been captivated by an extraordinary call to holiness on planet Earth.

The New Rebellion series is designed to equip us with powerful tools for partnering with God to change the world. That means a dichotomy of choices for the man or woman who wants to be a Christ-follower: Engaged or nonengaged. Effective or noneffective. Rebel with a cause or well-intentioned bystander in the spiritual struggle for a generation.

The New Rebellion movement is for those of us who are intensely passionate for Jesus and are determined to live a purposeful life. This pure passion is in stark contrast with the unholy passions of the earth. Those of us who embrace the

Rebellion have a fire in our eyes—a fire of love and triumph. We have a nothing-is-impossible mind-set. Jesus is not meek and mild to us; He is mighty and wild!

The New Rebellion generation is defined not by age or demographic. It includes the spiritually hungry of every age, culture, and gender who share a common passion to reach beyond a small life. It's time for courage and compassion to awaken a generation to its heavenly destiny. It's time for us to be who we're meant to be.

Book of Days is your daily source of perspective and courage to engage your world with purpose. God will empower you as you come into agreement with His agenda for your world each day. In one page, you will receive a verse or two rich with God's empowering vision. Then a few paragraphs of creative insight will light the fuse that will propel you into a day's worth of destiny. An affirming prayer at the conclusion will help you seal your resolve. Fifty-two weeks of inspiration and equipping.

Dare to join the New Rebellion!

Don't become so well-adjusted to your culture that you fit into it without even thinking. Instead, fix your attention on God. You'll be changed from the inside out.
Romans 12:2 MSG

It's quite simple: Do what is fair and just to your neighbor, be compassionate and loyal in your love, and don't take yourself too seriously—take God seriously.
Micah 6:8 MSG

day
1

We humans keep brainstorming options and plans, but GOD's purpose prevails.
Proverbs 19:21 MSG

Mental Block

Your mind, your body, your soul, your spirit—all are stamped with God's unchangeable purpose for your life. Life isn't about fashioning a purpose; it's about uncovering the custom-crafted purpose that has always existed for you in the mind of God.

And it's not a secret! More than anything else, God desires to convey to your heart an unshakable conviction of who you are (by His design), as well as your place in His big story. People run frantically through life "brainstorming options and plans" in a desperate attempt to be significant. But there is nothing more significant than trusting the good intentions of God.

Don't work so hard trying to figure it all out in your mind. God's not interested in giving you a divine road map without divine companionship. Pursue the relationship—He'll lead you into purpose.

God, I will trust Your plan for my life. And I will make Your face—not my plans—the center of my attention.

day 2

He thought of everything, provided for everything we could possibly need, letting us in on the plans he took such delight in making. He set it all out before us in Christ, a long-range plan in which everything would be brought together and summed up in him, everything in deepest heaven, everything on planet earth. Ephesians 1:8–10 MSG

The Whole World in His Hands

Your story is significant because it is part of His story. God's story. It's so amazing that He would include you in the New Rebellion, isn't it? He could do it all Himself, of course, but that would frustrate His whole intention in creating you. In creating the world.

Do you understand that you get to partner with God Himself? Into His long-range plan, He set you—at this very time and place—to play a part that no one else can play. If you believe that, then you'll throw aside the status quo and become an instigator of holy rebellion. Deepest heaven is coming to planet Earth . . . and you are an agent of transformation.

If you will own your role in this unfolding drama, He will let you in on the plan. And your vital role in it.

Purpose begins today. I will believe that God wants me to play a crucial part in His incredible plan for the world—my world—today.

day 3

The Scripture says to the Pharaoh, "For this very purpose I have raised you up, that I may show My power in you, and that My name may be declared in all the earth."
Romans 9:17 NKJV

Puppet Politics

There is no question that God is the power broker on planet Earth. Despite the very real presence of evil, there is a force that unrelentingly moves all people, all governments, all nations toward the ultimate purpose of God. And His power also moves your life!

If a stubborn, angry, arrogant man like Pharaoh could unwittingly become the very avenue for God to display His powerful love for His people so many years ago in Egypt (see Exodus 1–14), what do you think He can do with someone who loves Him and wants to be used by Him? Someone like you.

You were made for more than mere existence. Your heart tells you that you do indeed have a part to play in God's great agenda. Go for it! Don't let anyone tie you down to "normalcy."

God, I am not brilliant or powerful, but You are both.
So I will look for today's opportunities to reveal
Your greatness in ways large and small.

day 4

Declaring the end from the beginning, and from
ancient times things which have not been done,
saying, "My purpose will be established, and
I will accomplish all My good pleasure."
Isaiah 46:10 NASB

A Wrinkle in Time

Can God finish what He's started? Oh yeah.

Just as Jesus broke upon the earth as a rebel Himself in order to fulfill God's words from thousands of years earlier, so God knows exactly what He intends to do through your life. Of course, you're not a robot acting out some preprogrammed agenda. Instead, God placed all your desires and abilities and patterns of thinking inside one never-before-seen personality. One fascinating creation.

When your personality is given over to His direction, amazing things happen. Out of that intimate relationship, God leads you into the very purposes He thought up before the earth was even created. That's some brain strain, but it's true. Not even your mistakes and messes can hinder God's purpose in your life. If your heart belongs to Him, He makes your weaknesses the very platform for His strength.

God, thank You for Your declarations over my life so long ago.
I belong to You and will serve You all my days.

day
5

It is God who is working in you, [enabling you] both to will and to act for His good purpose.
Philippians 2:13 HCSB

The Chicken or the Egg?

Sometimes you don't really feel like doing God's purposes. Sometimes you'd rather take the path of least resistance and just be "normal." But that's not the real you! The real you can never settle for just fitting in. The real you rebels at the line of lemmings all walking in uniform brokenness toward futility. You are made for an extraordinary life!

At those times of wavering, God breathes upon the embers of your soul and ignites a new flame of passion and ability. To do the improbable. The impossible. And it is God Himself who activates both the "willing" and the "working." So which comes first, the desire or the ability? The answer: Whichever one He gives you first! Doing God's will increases your desire, and the desire leads you into more doing. Cool, huh?

God, You know how much I need Your strength to do Your purposes and to even want to do them. Remind me of who I am in You.

day 6

For this purpose I was appointed a herald and an apostle—I am telling the truth, I am not lying—and a teacher of the true faith to the Gentiles.
1 Timothy 2:7 NIV

Specificity

Knowing who you are and why you're here changes everything.

Paul's knowledge of his identity and purpose gave him the confidence and determination that were utterly essential to completing his mission. And though your mission may differ from his, you need the same confidence and determination to accomplish your purpose.

Don't settle for a vague idea of God's calling in your life—get specific! Ask God directly. Ask spiritual friends and spiritual authorities what they see in you. Look at your spiritual gifts; look at the kinds of things God has already authenticated in your life. Look at your longings.

In all these ways, let God's Spirit tell you who you are and why you're here. The world desperately needs you to come fully alive and live out your Kingdom purpose with confidence and determination.

God, infuse my soul with hope and courage to pursue Your specific calling on my life. Appoint me, send me, use me.

day
7

You followed God's prearranged plan. With the help of lawless Gentiles, you nailed him to the cross and murdered him.
Acts 2:23 NLT

A Prearranged Marriage

How could the most evil act in human history possibly be prearranged by God? Is God the author of evil? These are fair questions. And far from being mere philosophical musings, they bear directly upon your life: If God cannot be trusted on a cosmic level, why should you trust Him personally?

Let's start with the basics, with what *must* be true. God is a good God. The devil is a bad devil. God, in His wisdom, allowed the possibility for evil to enter earth. Having entered, evil will soon be conquered by the wisdom of God.

So how does that affect you? Simply this: Your heavenly Father is committed to bringing good results—every time!—from bad events in your life. If you will trust Him, even when it hurts, you will be empowered to live out the New Rebellion today.

God, I will trust You to marry bad experiences with good results in my life. You are committed to redeeming the places of suffering.

day 8

You're blessed when you've worked up a good appetite for God. He's food and drink in the best meal you'll ever eat.
Matthew 5:6 MSG

Bon Appétit

Sooner or later it will hit you: There is absolutely no thrill or pleasure as good as God. Nothing that compares to the satisfaction of His nearness, His engulfing love, and the joy of being His child.

You have lots of appetites—for food, for creativity, for conquest, for intimacy, to name a few. Every hunger you experience, as well as the experience that assuages your hunger, is a reflection of the Hunger. The overwhelming passion of your life—God Himself.

Your passion for Him is anchored in His passion for you. You didn't seek Him first; He chased you down, wrapped His big arms around you, and gave a joyous laugh of delight. And you fell in love, a great big love that you can never fall back out of. An endless sea of delight in your heavenly Papa!

God, all I want is Your grip on my heart. All I need is Your face in mine. All I want to do is feast my soul on You every day of my life.

day
9

If you try to keep your life for yourself, you will lose it. But if you give up your life for me, you will find true life.
Matthew 16:25 NLT

Abandon It

Paradox (par' a doks), n. a seemingly contradictory or absurd statement that expresses a possible truth.

There are lots of these with God, so you might as well get used to it! In the same way that the concept of negative numbers seems absurd to an eight-year-old, God's ways often seem to be nonsense. But they are, of course, the greatest sense of all.

Relinquishing your life completely to the care and control of Christ is a courageous leap of faith, a leap that takes the trust of a child. But once taken—once you accept the risk of losing everything that society holds up as valuable—then, and only then, will you be rewarded with Kingdom life. A life of no regret. A life worth living. A life that satisfies every yearning your soul possesses.

I abandon my life to You, God. I will lose myself in You and find all that really matters.

day 10

As the deer pants for streams of water, so my soul pants for you, O God. My soul thirsts for God, for the living God. When can I go and meet with God?
Psalm 42:1–2 NIV

Obey Your Thirst

God is the grandest addiction your soul can imagine. The more you taste, the more you hunger. The more you drink, the more you thirst.

Other addictions start out that way—addictions to entertainment, to food, to sports, or to busyness. But those addictions rob you blind while they perpetuate your slavery to their rule. The more you reach, the more of your soul you relinquish. It's a devilish plot that every person experiences in one form or another.

In stark contrast, the Rebel's thirst for God is more subtle, less demanding, but completely satisfying. You are not robbed, but enriched. Even as you are strengthened by God, your thirst deepens and widens until it becomes the context for all of life. And what a life it is. Rebel against lesser loves and choose the only thirst that will be fully quenched.

In the face of many choices, I choose life. I will feed my thirst for an extravagant love in God.

In the eighth year of his reign, while he was still young, he began to seek the God of his father David; and in the twelfth year he began to purge Judah and Jerusalem of the high places, the wooden images, the carved images, and the molded images.
2 Chronicles 34:3 NKJV

day
11

Purging Passion

The same passion that draws your heart hard after God also pushes your heart hard away from false gods. If that dynamic is not in place, then passion is not yet fully formed. The verse above describes a remarkable young man named Josiah who became king at the age of eight! The Bible then describes how he turned his heart toward God and changed the destiny of a nation. Just like you!

Four years later, Josiah began to purge all the idolatry from his country. Today's idols are more subtle but no less real. Do you know the things, the activities, or the affections that seek first place in your heart? Does your passion for God lead you to declare war on those challengers or do you give them some room? This is a time for vigilance, not passivity!

Today, my passion for God will guard the throne of my heart from all usurpers and keep it for Him only.

day 12

Whom have I in heaven but You? And besides You,
I desire nothing on earth. My flesh and my heart
may fail, but God is the strength of my
heart and my portion forever.
Psalm 73:25–26 NASB

Windfall Inheritance

If you were to suddenly receive a huge inheritance, you'd probably stop clipping coupons for groceries. Your new abundance would mean you wouldn't have to worry about nickels and dimes anymore. No more scraping to get by. And so it is—this is your reality!

In the light of all the enormous wealth of who God is and His lavish generosity to you, what earthly things are now compelling? What lack could there possibly be? His beauty is all-encompassing, His fellowship intoxicating. His resource is now your only source, your only strength, your only passion.

Your weaknesses and failures that defined your past have lost their grip on you. His excellence is now yours. Your name is on the will. Everything He is and has belongs to you! You are fully equipped to change your world through the New Rebellion.

God, may my passion today be fueled by Your extravagant love for me and Your supply for my every need.

day 13

"Get these out of here! How dare you turn my Father's house into a market!" His disciples remembered that it is written: "Zeal for your house will consume me."

John 2:16–17 NIV

Tap into Heaven's Passion

There is a common misperception in Christian circles that godliness is demonstrated by being meek and mild. Not so. While humility and gentleness are authentic virtues in God's Word, so are courage and zeal. And God's Rebel knows *when* to operate in each!

With honest seekers, Jesus was invariably gentle and approachable, no matter how broken their lives. But when it came to those who promoted their own profit and wielded their own control—in the name of God—Jesus was absolutely fierce.

While mercy and compassion may occupy 99 percent of your interaction with others, there is a time for passionate confrontation with evil that masquerades as good. Even then, remember that your real confrontation is with the spiritual world (see Ephesians 6:12). Yes, there will be times when your passion for God will require you to stand courageously for truth.

God, help me to represent You well this day, knowing when to be quiet and when to be loud on Your behalf.

day 14

If you love Me, you will keep My commandments.
John 14:15 HCSB

Passion Shows

Can you hear Jesus' bold, simple call echoing across the crowds, "Come, follow Me"? It was a warm invitation, but also a forceful challenge. One that required a decisive response. This same universal call now echoes across the generations with incisive power. Today, you may not have Jesus as a person to follow around, but you have His truth, His ways, and His Spirit to devote your life to.

When you decide to step out and follow Him, a flame of passion grows in your heart. Your love for Him is demonstrated in the radical way you live your life. In following Jesus you see redemptive transformation in all your relationships, your plans, your job, your finances. The simple truth is that His ways work, and once you choose a life of obedience, you will never be the same again!

God, You see my passion to follow You. Let my life now demonstrate the extent of my devotion to You.

day 15

Don't become so well-adjusted to your culture that you fit into it without even thinking. Instead, fix your attention on God. You'll be changed from the inside out.

Romans 12:2 MSG

Radical Times Call for Radical Living

In the early days of God's people, when a man or woman wanted to make a public declaration of radical subjection to the purposes of God, they took a spiritual vow to be a Nazirite. For a period of time, or for a lifetime, these men and women lived a life of consecration to God. In diet and appearance—notably an abstention from cutting their hair!—they proclaimed that one thing, and one thing alone, was the sole focus of their attention: God.

In these days God is calling you to arise as a new generation of spiritual Nazirites! Instead of being recognized by hair or food, your generation will be known by an inner fire that burns with unrelenting passion and purity. You will not defile yourself with the trivial pursuits of your contemporary culture; instead, your life will be constantly shaped by another culture—God's Kingdom culture.

God, I dedicate myself to Your purposes this day. I will be a spiritual Nazirite, immune to the whims of this culture and fascinated by You alone!

day 16

The LORD has rewarded me according to my
righteousness, according to my cleanness in
his sight . . . To the pure you show yourself pure,
but to the crooked you show yourself shrewd.
2 Samuel 22:25, 27 NIV

Purity Is Magnetic

Purity is not something you work up by your own effort to impress God or earn His favor. He has already set His favor upon you because He's impressed with His Son, Jesus. And because of His overwhelming commitment to you, He invites you into His purity and then gives you the ability to walk in it. Purity powers the New Rebellion!

One of many cool things about purity is that it's magnetic—it draws the blessings of God to your life with powerful force. This passage describes how purity brings reward, and one of those rewards is a revelation of God Himself, specifically an illumination of *His* purity and holiness. And this is a priceless gift. By the way, impurity is also magnetic; it draws lots of bad stuff to you that you don't want to deal with.

God, there's no one as awesome as You! You give me the desire for a clean heart, then You clean my heart, and then You reward me on top of that!

day
17

The lamp of the body is the eye. If therefore your eye is good, your whole body will be full of light.
Matthew 6:22 NKJV

Glow

The challenge and the opportunity of every Christ-follower is to be single-minded in pursuit of God, not distracted by lesser things. The result of this degree of focus in life is purity. To illustrate this theme, Jesus gave a powerful analogy about the eye as the lamp of the body: What enters your soul through your eyes will either illumine your heart or darken it. So which will it be?

God's calling on your life is to change your world. To be fully released into that destiny requires maximum illumination, maximum clarity. You don't want to be blinded by impure distractions, stumbling around making foolish choices. Television, movies, advertisements, newspapers, environments—each of these sources will either brighten or darken your passion for God. Choose wisely and shine brightly! The Rebellion needs you.

I choose to focus my attention today on things that are pure and true so that I can live in the brilliance of God's fellowship and purpose.

day 18

The mouth speaks out of that which fills the heart.
Matthew 12:34 NASB

Mouth Freshener

Nobody likes bad breath, but negative conversation lingers even longer in the heart than odors in the air. You wouldn't willingly offend people's noses, so why would you offend their ears with oppressive words and attitudes contrary to the Kingdom? Sometimes it's easier to freshen your breath than to purify your heart, but it's the heart that's the issue.

You don't always even know what is in your heart until the words pop out of your mouth. So your words need to be taken seriously; they don't come from nowhere. Jesus is saying in this passage that your words are an expression of the condition of your heart. The goal here is not primarily to change the words, but to change your heart! Don't get sidetracked trying to cure the symptom when you can redeem the source.

God, I can't change my own heart, but You can. Wash away all the germs of my soul so that my words and my presence bring Your life!

day 19

How can a young person live a clean life?
By carefully reading the map of your Word.
Psalm 119:9 MSG

It's Okay to Ask for Directions

Your life does not come with an instruction manual or a road map; however, your life with Christ does. All the dead-end streets that confuse and sidetrack so many in life are clearly indicated on God's road map, His Word. More important, He charts out the highway to purity and destiny. Rebels who diligently study the map rarely get lost.

But God has given you even more than a map; He's given you a GPS! Before Jesus left planet Earth, He said He would send you His Spirit to remind you of His words and keep you oriented in your journey. He knew that you would regularly need His direction, but sometimes forget to pick up the map. So the Spirit becomes an internal positioning system to point the way to purity and warn you of obstructions.

I'm asking for Your directions this day, God. I trust Your wisdom to chart my course and lead me into a pure and unhindered destiny.

day 20

Create in me a pure heart, O God, and renew a steadfast spirit within me. Do not cast me from your presence or take your Holy Spirit from me.
Psalm 51:10 NIV

Rechargeable

No matter how strong your desire for God, there are times when you mess up, when you make foolish choices and trade the rewards of purity for the heaviness of a guilty conscience. In those dark moments, your heart intuitively wonders if God's commitment to you still stands or if you've ticked Him off a little too much. Maybe your glorious future in God is uncertain. Maybe you've gone too far.

But there is one cry that is never denied: "Don't cast me from Your presence, Lord! Don't abandon me. You are my only hope." As King David, who wrote this poignant psalm, discovered, the best Father of all rushes to cleanse the soul wounded by sin. He grabs you up, not in vengeful anger, but in a redeeming bear hug. And in one heavenly instant, He restores the purity of your heart.

Thank You, God, for not throwing me away like a used-up battery. Recharge me and restore me with Your life-giving grace.

Dear friends, we are God's children now, and what we will be has not yet been revealed. We know that when He appears, we will be like Him, because we will see Him as He is. And everyone who has this hope in Him purifies himself just as He is pure.
1 John 3:2–3 HCSB

day 21

Leading the Base

One of the things that makes God God is the transforming effect He has upon His children. He is, at the core, a redeemer of broken lives and a restorer of beauty. And He uses "rebuilt" people to advance His cause in the earth. This is both a future hope and a present reality. How does that work?

All of history is moving toward one inescapable conclusion: the establishing of the fullness of God's rule over all things. When that happens all the earth will see Him in the unfiltered brilliance of His unbearable beauty. And that sight will utterly transform you into the beauty for which you were created. But it begins now! Every glimpse you get now brings incremental transformation of your soul.

This is His incredible invitation to you: Step off the base. Get a head start!

Today I'm going to lead the base and move toward the goal of more of Your beauty in my life. Show me Yourself this day.

day 22

When you pray, don't be like the hypocrites who love to pray publicly on street corners and in the synagogues where everyone can see. I assure you, that is all the reward they will ever get.
Matthew 6:5 NLT

Private Practice

What part does prayer play in the New Rebellion? What is prayer supposed to be like and who is it really for? When you pray aloud in a group, are your words for them or for God? Do you find yourself rehearsing your prayers or trying to sound intelligent?

Prayer is not a show; it's not a litmus test to see how spiritual you are. Jesus was very clear about that! Prayer is a personal conversation with Someone who already knows and loves you thoroughly. Prayer is a powerful way to change the planet.

So, no matter who else is listening, pray for an audience of one. Be free to pour out your thoughts, worries, fears, and needs with unvarnished honesty. Your words establish an intimate and empowering connection that changes both you and your world.

God, I want to be real with You. Help me just to say what I need to say, to listen for Your reply, and move with You in the world.

The moment we get tired in the waiting, God's Spirit is right alongside helping us along. If we don't know how or what to pray, it doesn't matter. He does our praying in and for us, making prayer out of our wordless sighs, our aching groans.
Romans 8:26 MSG

day 23

Groaning and Sighing

God's Spirit was the answer to Jesus' promise before He left for heaven. The Spirit brings everything you need—the ability to pray, the ability to live. When you face situations that are so complicated you don't even know what to ask for, stop and let God's Spirit talk to the Father about it. When you are too tired to speak coherent words, stop and let the Spirit utter them for you. When you are too upset to pray, just pause and let Him communicate heaven's will.

The Spirit who now lives in you knows every detail of what God intends to do in your life. So let the weary sighs, the frustrated groans, and the desperate cries of "Help me, God" flow out! The Spirit will interpret your heart and bring you into alignment with heaven's purpose in your world.

God, thank You for sending Your Spirit to live inside me. Now rule my heart and pray Your heart as we partner together.

day 24

Be joyful always; pray continually; give thanks in all circumstance, for this is God's will for you in Christ Jesus.
1 Thessalonians 5:16–18 NIV

Perpetuate Your Prayers

Did you know that the little conversations you have in your head are simply prayers in formation?

When you are going about your day and you find your mind wandering to issues of anxiety or problems you can't solve, this is an unexpected invitation to intimacy. Turn those thoughts and emotions into prayer. Instead of becoming agitated or fixated on a problem, convey them to God and release the weight. This is continuous prayer.

In this way, prayer becomes as natural and constant as breath itself. The breath of life, the breath of the New Rebellion. Your eyes don't need to be closed; your head doesn't need to be bowed. Prayer is simply your intimate conversation with the Father. Thanksgiving flows out of a heart that walks in the reality of a big God.

God, turn my head noise into prayer this day
so that every problem becomes an invitation
to thanksgiving and renewal for Your purposes.

[Jesus] then told them a parable on the need for them to pray always and not become discouraged.
Luke 18:1 HCSB

Don't Quit!

The story Jesus told on the need for the disciples to pray was about a heartless judge who ignored a widow in desperate need. The judge relented and came to her aid only because she wouldn't quit hounding him for help. So what about you? Do you give up easily in prayer or do you persevere until your prayer is answered?

Your God is the farthest thing from heartless; He is a caring Father who diligently provides for His kids! He listens to every cry, every need of your heart, spoken or unspoken. Your view of Him will show whether you trust His heart or not.

Frequently His timing is different from yours. When you don't get the results you're looking for, you're tempted to doubt His goodness and give up the quest. Don't do it! The heart of this parable is to find courage and bring change.

God, I trust Your heart toward me, and I won't ever give up on You. You inspire and empower me to pray with courage and constancy.

day 26

Is anyone among you suffering? Then he must pray. Is anyone cheerful? He is to sing praises. Is anyone among you sick? Then he must call for the elders of the church and they are to pray over him, anointing him with oil in the name of the Lord.
James 5:13–14 NASB

Going Public

Authority is a powerful force for blessing in your life. The men and women who have leadership roles in your community of faith are an avenue of God's protection and nurture in your soul. Don't hesitate to ask for prayer for healing and miracles. The supernatural is biblical Christianity, and it is the lifeblood of the New Rebellion.

A community who prays is an essential environment for spiritual growth and transformation. Be transparent enough and bold enough to invite prayer, not just for stubbed toes but also for cancer and for every threat of death. God has joined you to others to release His power.

Let God's authority move through your agreement. Take the risk to pray for others' sickness and suffering. God is a big God with big plans for you. Enlarge your view of Him and Let Him restore others through your prayers.

God, I know that You want to heal every place of pain and destruction. Let Your healing grace flow to me and through me to others.

day 27

I tell you that if two of you on earth agree about anything you ask for, it will be done for you by my Father in heaven. For where two or three come together in my name, there am I with them.
Matthew 18:19–20 NIV

Dynamic Duos

It is a universal law that unity brings power. The human will is a gift from God and a potent tool for either evil or good. Turned against the will of God, it becomes destructive and invites the judgment of Babel's tower (see Genesis 11). But brought into agreement with the will of God—and the will of spiritual friends—your will brings God-sized results!

Although God doesn't need your agreement to do what He wants to do, His great desire is to move in partnership with you for Kingdom purposes. He wants to bring the Kingdom of heaven to earth, so when He places the heartbeat of heaven inside your chest, heaven and earth come into agreement and God's power is released through your prayers. Community satisfies the heart of God—and your heart—like nothing else.

God, as I gather to pray with my family and friends today, show us Your heart so that we can agree together with You.

day 28

Who can climb Mount GOD? Who can scale the holy north-face? Only the clean-handed, only the pure-hearted.
Psalm 24:3–4 MSG

Access Is for the Adventurous

Anyone can open his mouth, say words, and call it a prayer. But those prayers may not move the heart of God in any way. Those who *move* the heart of God are those who *know* the heart of God.

Effectiveness in prayer is the domain of those who have made it their life's pursuit to know God and live in His presence. You don't have to be a monk. You don't have to be brilliant. But there is a serious quest, a searching, a pursuit that requires energy and attention. It isn't for the faint of heart!

If you set your sights on purity, taking advantage of God's ready forgiveness, then you will be unhindered in your quest to "climb Mount GOD." Your time in His presence will bring you into agreement with Him and empower the Rebellion.

I will be a spiritual adventurer. I will not be a casual Christian. By knowing Your heart, my prayers will change the world.

day 29

This saying is trustworthy: "If anyone aspires to be an overseer, he desires a noble work." An overseer, therefore, must be above reproach.
1 Timothy 3:1–2 HCSB

A Worthy Pursuit

Are you a noble person? That may sound like a strange question, but God is very interested in noble women and men. He's interested in your nobility! Nobility is found in those who take risks for a righteous cause without selfish ambition. Nobility requires leadership, and effective leadership requires nobility.

It is the unworthy pursuit of selfish goals that, beyond all else, undermines that nobility and brings reproach upon leadership. Nobility sets aside personal desires and advancement for the privilege of serving others and leading them toward a worthy goal. This is the quality of character that will change the world, and this is the caliber of leadership that must fuel God's Rebels who seek His Kingdom.

Your leadership may flow in a very small sphere of influence, but it is the quality, not the extent, of your leadership that releases nobility.

My leadership matters, and I take seriously the privilege of serving God and others at home, at school or work, and in the church.

Leadership

day 30

Since we have gifts that differ according to the grace given to us, each of us is to exercise them accordingly: . . . he who leads, with diligence. Romans 12:6–8 NASB

Find Your Grace Gift

To lead effectively requires you to know yourself. Specifically, effective leadership requires you to know the gifts and the abilities, the strengths and the weaknesses that God placed within you. Often, the best way to discover your gifts, whether spiritual or natural, is to track the trail of *grace* in your life.

Grace is like oil—it reduces friction and brings ease of movement. There are certain functions in your soul that God has graced with divine "oil." These are the things that flow without so much effort, and these are the gifts you should cultivate within your sphere of leadership. Sometimes, life requires you to move outside your area of grace, but wise Kingdom Rebels keep moving back toward their grace gifting. This will bring life to you and empower your leadership with God's favor and blessing.

God, help me to lead diligently, using the grace You have deposited in my soul to bring out the best in those I serve.

Your kingdom will not endure; the LORD has sought out a man after his own heart and appointed him leader of his people, because you have not kept the LORD'S command.
1 Samuel 13:14 NIV

day 31

Ability Is Not Enough

The story of King Saul is a tragic one, and one that contains a great lesson for all leaders. Saul's leadership gift lay dormant until the prophet Samuel anointed him king and practically forced leadership upon him. At that point, Saul began to grow rapidly into a powerful leader. Sadly, though, he did not grow into a godly one.

Leadership *ability* is not enough to advance the cause of Christ in the earth. As Saul discovered the hard way, it takes a man or a woman whose heart burns with the things of God's heart. Does yours?

God will trust you as a leader only when He knows that you care about the people and the purposes that He values. He always resists proud leaders who lead for their own benefit, but if you pursue God's vision with your leadership, He will equip and empower you!

God, make me a person after Your own heart. I want to be motivated by the things and the people You care about.

day 32

Deborah, a prophetess, the wife of Lappidoth, was leading Israel at that time.
Judges 4:4 NIV

God May Surprise You!

Sometimes you don't choose leadership; leadership may choose you!

In the time of the judges in Israel, a woman named Deborah was serving the people as a prophetic leader. Anyone who had a dispute with another person would come to her court for a decision. When God spoke that it was time for the Israelites to throw off the cruel oppression of the Canaanites, Deborah called a man named Barak to lead the army.

Confronted with Barak's lack of confidence, she knew she must rise to the occasion and go with the army herself. She did not choose this task; it chose her. Don't be surprised if God places you in a situation you would never have chosen, a situation that requires your leadership. If it's God doing the calling, then you can be bold and fierce as a leader.

God, give me the courage to lead when You call me to it. Let my weakness be the very avenue of Your strength.

day 33

Joshua fell with his face to the ground in reverence. "I am at your command," Joshua said. "What do you want your servant to do?"
Joshua 5:14 NLT

Command Is Delegated

The power of a leader does not flow from his or her skill or force of personality. True leadership flows out of a delegated commission. In other words, your greatest asset as a leader rests in the authority and the responsibility communicated to you by your leader—your parents, your boss, your teacher, your pastor, or your God.

Knowing where your responsibility comes from equips you to know both the goals and boundaries of your leadership. This brings confidence and humility, which are essential qualities for any leader. When you know the source of your authority, you can move confidently to fulfill the tasks assigned to you and not move beyond them.

Joshua was the leader of all Israel, but he understood that his every action was accountable to God. This empowered him to effectively lead God's people into their inheritance.

Help me, God, to honor the authorities in my life by rightly using the authority that has been delegated to me.

day 34

He rejected the counsel of the elders and asked the young men he'd grown up with who were now currying his favor, "What do you think? What should I say to these people who are saying, 'Give us a break from your father's harsh ways—lighten up on us'?"
1 Kings 12:8–9 MSG

Company Speaks Volumes

In the recent movie *Troy,* the king of Troy twice fails to listen to his two sons and instead follows the advice of his old advisers. Both decisions lead to death. In the same way, King Rehoboam took the advice of his friends over the counsel of those who knew him and knew God best.

To lead wisely—in any area of life—you must have trusted friends, proven allies, comrades-in-arms who are able to speak into your life and into the hard decisions you face. In those times, you sometimes *want* people to say what you already think, but wise advisers will always speak the truth, even when it's unpopular. God puts people in your life to challenge you and, more important, to illuminate your blind spots. Sometimes it all comes down to knowing who to listen to.

God, I'm glad You made me a leader. I need the wise people You have put around me, and I choose to be humble and listen to them.

David had a craving and said, "Oh that someone would give me water to drink from the well of Bethlehem which is by the gate!" So the three mighty men broke through the camp of the Philistines.
2 Samuel 23:15–16 NASB

day 35

Affection and Devotion

You can be a reasonably decent leader and have people obey you. But when those you lead both love and respect you, then you have something priceless! King David was such a leader.

He was locked in battle against a huge enemy and happened to give voice to his craving for a cool drink. He would never have commanded his men to steal into enemy country for such a thing. But the power of David's leadership lay in the affection he had earned from his men. So his three top commanders risked their lives to bring him that drink of water!

What about you? Are those who look to you for leadership devoted to you? Will they take risks to protect you and provide for you? The answer to that question will speak volumes about the quality of your leadership.

God, help me to be devoted to those I lead and earn their trust and affection. Build a bond among us of mutual dedication.

day 36

Drink the Spirit of God, huge draughts of him. Sing hymns instead of drinking songs! Sing songs from your heart to Christ. Sing praises over everything, any excuse for a song to God the Father in the name of our Master, Jesus Christ.
Ephesians 5:18–20 MSG

Bottoms Up

When God designed and created you, He had one overarching purpose in mind: that you would be capable of loving and worshipping Him in a way all your own. You are made for worship. Every cell in your body comes alive and confirms its truest destiny when your face turns toward His in wholehearted adoration.

His presence will refresh you more than a cool glass of water on a hot day. His nearness will intoxicate your soul with a gladness beyond words. Then it will well up inside you like a song and take words that are just busting to get out. So give expression to your passion! Sing, bow, clap, dance. Convey your delight in His beauty using every expression that flows out of your heart. Then turn your worship loose to serve others and serve God.

God, I will take every opportunity, any excuse, to lift my heart to You in praise today. Fill my mouth with grateful songs.

O Nebuchadnezzar, we do not need to defend ourselves before you. If we are thrown into the blazing furnace, the God whom we serve is able to save us. He will rescue us from your power, Your Majesty. But even if he doesn't, Your Majesty can be sure that we will never serve your gods.
Daniel 3:16–18 NLT

day
37

Fearless in the Fire 1

Your worship is the most valuable possession you own. It should not be given away lightly, and it certainly should not be given to any pretender-gods, no matter how many people are lined up at their altar. New Rebellion worshippers are fearless in worship, dedicated to bringing their sacrifice to only One. No matter the cost.

And there is a cost, generally measured in terms of intimidation and rejection from popular culture, as Daniel and his friends found out. The current of worship in this generation generally flows in the direction of self, and the only ones willing to swim against that current are those who are captivated by another love, a higher passion. A revelation of the actual worth-ship of God is a compelling force and brings courage to resist the dictates of social conformity.

Open the eyes of my heart, God, to see Your awesomeness. Captivate my heart and keep my affections for You only!

day 38

I urge you, brethren, by the mercies of God, to present your bodies a living and holy sacrifice, acceptable to God, which is your spiritual service of worship.
Romans 12:1 NASB

Fearless in the Fire 2

Are you ready to be a human sacrifice? Doesn't sound too appealing, does it? What could God have been thinking when He made this the description of authentic worship?

First, real worship is all or nothing. It's not just something you do; it's an all-encompassing identity and commitment. God isn't interested in just a piece of your heart—He deserves the whole thing. Second, sacrifice does involve a bit of pain from time to time. There is a dying to selfish interests, a dying to a life that offers comfort and affirmation from this world.

But the rewards far exceed any pain you'll experience. For example, the pain of having your bike stolen would probably be eased by someone giving you a new car! Or as Paul says, "I don't think there's any comparison between the present hard times and the coming good times" (Romans 8:18 MSG).

God, I want to belong to You lock, stock, and barrel—nothing held back, nothing in reserve. I am Yours completely.

day 39

Your worship must engage your spirit in the pursuit of truth. That's the kind of people the Father is out looking for: those who are simply and honestly themselves before him in their worship . . . Those who worship him must do it out of their very being, their spirits, their true selves, in adoration.
John 4:23–24 MSG

Transparency

Do you know your heart? No one knows themselves completely . . . but God does. And the invitation of God is to bring your whole self—the good, the bad, and the ugly—into an honest and transparent pursuit of God.

God's not into playing religious games. You can't impress Him like you can sometimes impress people. The quest to worship God will require an unveiling of your heart, a breaking of masks and pretenses, so that you acknowledge your own brokenness in order to obtain His healing and reconstruction.

God's call to Spirit-worship takes this far beyond the activity of your mind and mere belief into the deepest place—the place designed for supernatural encounter. Your authentic pursuit of God will cause you to know yourself better . . . and to bow that self before His majesty.

Help me to stop pretending, God, to stop trying to be someone I'm not. You want the real me, and so that's what I bring to You today.

day 40

I envied the arrogant when I saw the prosperity of the wicked. They have no struggles . . . They are free from the burdens common to man . . . When I tried to understand all this, it was oppressive to me till I entered the sanctuary of God; then I understood their final destiny.
Psalm 73:3–5, 16–17 NIV

Perspective!

You've heard that timing is everything. Try perspective! Your perspective of God, your perspective of yourself, the church, the world—these perspectives, whether accurate or not, will define your life and future.

One of the big hurdles that every Christ-follower has to cross from time to time is the feeling that godliness just isn't worth it. Let's be honest. Sometimes it feels like character isn't worth it. Like sacrifice and discipline don't really pay off. It's easy to look around and see people finding great money, prestige, and recognition who couldn't care less about the things of God.

The psalm writer found this thought oppressive until he got into God's presence and found one thing: perspective! *Oh yeah, God, those guys are going to lose everything sooner or later. But I have You, so I have everything. And I'll never lose it!*

God, give me Your Kingdom perspective on my life and my world so I can have the confidence to pursue what really matters.

day 41

[Satan] said to [Jesus], "All these things I will give You if You will fall down and worship me." Then Jesus said to him, "Away with you, Satan! For it is written, 'You shall worship the LORD your God, and Him only you shall serve.'"
Matthew 4:9–10 NKJV

All These Things

Satan wasn't very subtle when Jesus was being tempted in the desert. Sometimes he's a lot more subtle with you, but his agenda is exactly the same. He wants to buy you! Can you be bought?

Can your allegiance, your affection, your time, your money, your energy be purchased and transferred from the things of the Kingdom to the things of this world? Time will surely tell. The traitor in the movie *The Matrix* got tired of the difficulties in the real world and chose to go back to the fake virtual world just because it was more comfortable.

Jesus used the classic comparison between the broad, easy road leading to destruction and the narrow road leading to life. But it keeps coming back to perspective, doesn't it. Who is really worth the worship of your life?

Every day I see it more clearly: the things Satan offers me are worthless, but the treasures of God are priceless!

day 42

Wherever the gospel is proclaimed in the whole world, what this woman has done will also be told in memory of her.
Mark 14:9 HCSB

Extravagance

Do you know which story Jesus is referring to here? Mary of Bethany, sister of Martha and Lazarus, had just done something shocking—something seemingly wasteful and extravagant. While Jesus was eating dinner, Mary poured a jar full of perfumed oil onto His head, a rare oil that cost a year's wages!

Some were indignant and began to criticize Mary for being so inappropriate. There was obviously a great disparity of perspective there. Jesus saw that this woman perceived the real values of the Kingdom of God. In fact, she recognized Jesus' worth beyond anyone else present, and she did the most obviously natural thing: She lavished her best on Him.

This is precisely the heart of worship. And it so accurately reflects God's heart that Jesus declared it would be told everywhere and be part of the very gospel message.

God, I want to see the worth of Your Son and be captivated by Him so that everything I have and am is poured out for Him!

day 43

Oh yes, you shaped me first inside, then out; you formed me in my mother's womb . . . The days of my life all prepared before I'd even lived one day.
Psalm 139:13, 16 MSG

You Are a Miracle

Isn't it great to be totally known? It is an amazing thought that the Creator of this big wide world created you. God knows every little detail about who you are and what makes you tick.

The Creator thought, *Cool, I'll give this one red hair, green eyes, and a gift of giving; that one I'm going to make short and agile with a knack for sports and a love for justice!* God loves who you are, and you need to love who you are too. Tell God how happy you are with the good work of His hands, that everything He accomplishes is perfect!

When you can trust the wisdom of God in creating you as He did—really grateful for His work in you—then you can trust the future He has prepared for you as well.

God, I embrace the life You have prepared for me. I don't know what lies ahead, but I know it will be good because You are good.

day 44

You shall love your neighbor as yourself:
I am the LORD.
Leviticus 19:18 NKJV

Love Yourself?

Love yourself? Doesn't sound very spiritual! In fact, it sounds downright contrary to a lot of Christian teaching that's around. It must just be the latest pop psychology . . . except that it's in the Bible. Oops.

This commandment from Moses about loving your neighbor was echoed many years later by Jesus Himself. When Jesus summed up the entire Old Testament law in one sentence—Love God!—He felt compelled to tack on this addendum: "Love God *and* love your neighbor."

But then the qualification is that you must love your neighbor with the same quality and to the same extent you love *yourself*. Whoa! The implication is clear: If you don't love yourself well, then you can't love another well. The refusal to accept God's goodness displayed in you will undermine your ability to appreciate God's goodness displayed in others.

God, I want to love the people You've placed in my world, so help me to love all the works of Your hands, beginning with me.

day
45

You're blessed when you're content with just who you are—no more, no less.
Matthew 5:5 MSG

Satisfaction Guaranteed

God loves to give surprises. How are you on receiving them? When you receive the gift of yourself with a thankful and content heart, then you'll be able to see the beauty of His design. This means being happy with both the outward and inward pieces that make up "you." You're still a work in progress, but it's essential to be satisfied with what He put in you and what He left out.

Don't cut yourself short wishing for another gift or a different body. Be aware of what you can do for God with what He has given. It's a very simple but extraordinarily powerful force to accept the goodness of God as demonstrated in you. To fight your identity is to paralyze destiny; to own your God-given identity is to move boldly into your future as a Kingdom Rebel.

God, I submit to who You have made me to be. Even with all my imperfections I choose to serve You. It's all good. Even me!

day
46

The LORD said to Samuel, "Don't judge by his appearance or height, for I have rejected him. The LORD doesn't make decisions the way you do! People judge by outward appearance, but the LORD looks at a person's thoughts and intentions."
1 Samuel 16:7 NLT

Go for the Core

Isn't it refreshing that God doesn't look at you the way people do? Men and women form their first opinion of someone by what they see on the outside—the way they're dressed, the car they drive, their education or wealth. But the New Rebellion looks deeper, for the hidden value of people to emerge.

Even Samuel, God's prophet, got caught up in appearances when it came time to anoint a king. God had to tell him, "Cut that out! I know Jesse's other sons look impressive, but the one who loves Me best is not at all impressive on the outside. When I look at David, his heart speaks to Me, not his face. I value who he is becoming, not how strong or handsome he is. I love that his heart is tender and listens to Me."

God, I long to see with Your eyes. Help me to not be swayed by appearances but by the heart. I want to look deeper and see what's real.

day 47

Your beauty should not consist of outward things [like] elaborate hairstyles and the wearing of gold ornaments or fine clothes; instead, [it should consist of] the hidden person of the heart with the imperishable quality of a gentle and quiet spirit, which is very valuable in God's eyes.
1 Peter 3:3–4 HCSB

Extreme Makeovers

Guys and girls of all ages face the pressures of outward conformity to this world's dictates, whether the pressures are hairstyles, clothes, and body piercings or houses, cars, and portfolios. But your worth comes from a higher, holier place—the one source of lasting beauty, God Himself. He seeks those who will throw down false idols of vanity and insecurity in order to embrace a profound heavenly ownership.

God's extreme makeover begins in the heart. When you invest your greatest resources—your time, your money, and your passion—in the cultivation of the inner life, your image becomes His image. And that is some kind of beautiful! Holiness is attractive, drawing those with broken self-images to the Healer of all hearts.

When your inside radiates the beauty of God, then your outer appearance begins to come into agreement. You become a heavenly fashion statement!

God, I choose to forsake the meaningless standards of worldly beauty in order to discover Your awesome intentions for my life, inside and out.

day 48

Joshua was dressed in filthy clothes as he stood before the angel. The angel said to those who were standing before him, "Take off his filthy clothes." Then he said to Joshua, "See, I have taken away your sin, and I will put rich garments on you."
Zechariah 3:3–4 NIV

Change Your Clothes

Joshua had an identity problem. No, not that Joshua. This was Joshua the high priest who returned from Babylon to Jerusalem, along with Ezra and Nehemiah, to rebuild the Temple. The problem was, after getting the foundations laid, they were forced to stop work . . . for almost twenty years!

It's so easy to get your identity wrapped up in what you do and not in who you are! But not so for God's Rebels. In the middle of Joshua's depression, the prophet Zechariah had a vision of encouragement: In it, an angel challenged him to take off his filthy clothes. They weren't literal clothes, of course; they represented his faulty image of himself.

In order for Joshua to see God's power released and the Temple built, he had to see himself the way God saw him . . . in the "rich garments" of God's favor and delight.

Okay, I'm ready, God. Strip away my distorted self-image that's based on what I do. I'm ready to clothe myself in Your favor!

"Your name will no longer be Jacob," the man told him. "It is now Israel, because you have struggled with both God and men and have won."
Genesis 32:28 NLT

day 49

A New Name

Jacob's journey to obtain his true identity was long and arduous. The fact that his name meant "deceiver" didn't help! He lived up to his name for many years, even though he really did have a heart for God.

Finally, God knew it was time and sent an angel who wrestled with Jacob throughout an entire night. This literal wrestling match was symbolic of Jacob's lifelong struggle to understand his own soul and his calling in life. Eventually, the two wrestlers came to a stalemate, and Jacob challenged this mysterious figure to bless him.

Of all things, the blessing God gave Jacob was a new name, representative of his new identity and new destiny. And from that time on, Jacob was free to obey God in a whole new capacity. True identity is imperative in the New Rebellion.

God, I don't want to have to wrestle an angel! Just tell me who I am and what You have for me to do. It's my joy to obey You.

day 50

Have I not commanded you? Be strong and courageous. Do not be terrified; do not be discouraged, for the LORD your God will be with you wherever you go.
Joshua 1:9 NIV

Strength in Transition

When God spoke these words to Joshua, he was in a particularly awkward and emotional transition. His mentor of more than forty years had just died, and he had just assumed command of roughly a million Jews. There was no time for the slow development of leadership skills; he was faced with the immediate task of conquering a land that was stronger than they in every way.

These are times that require great courage and confidence in God. Perhaps you, too, face a situation that requires great courage. God's charge to Joshua also applies to you: Your unstoppable strength will flow out of your obedience to God's directions. Oh, and one more thing—you're not alone! You can step forward into your destiny with the certainty that God Himself goes with you. His strength is now your strength.

I will not be terrified or discouraged with the impossible circumstances I face. With God all things are possible.

day 51

I live in eager expectation and hope that I will never do anything that causes me shame, but that I will always be bold for Christ, as I have been in the past, and that my life will always honor Christ, whether I live or I die.
Philippians 1:20 NLT

Bold in Life, Bold in Death

The man or woman who trusts God fully is unstoppable! Death holds no fear, and life holds no intimidation.

Hope is the happy condition of the soul that is seized by clarity and confidence—*clarity* that your resources (God and all His supply) far exceed your challenges, and *confidence* that God's calling in your life is backed up by His commitment to your welfare. These convictions of the heart will release the same "eager expectation" Paul experienced, an expectation that good things await you, that you will not be ashamed, and that Christ will be honored by all your deeds.

In other words, you can afford to be bold! Not because you know everything that's going to happen, but because you know who's in charge of it all. He is trustworthy, and He will work powerfully through you.

God, send me out into this day with the same clarity and confidence Paul had. After all, we have the same God behind us.

day 52

Be alert, stand firm in the faith, be brave and strong. Your every [action] must be done with love.
1 Corinthians 16:13–14 HCSB

The Motivation for Your Action

You might not have considered before the connection between love and courage. In this passage, Paul encourages the Corinthian Christians to be brave and loving in the same breath. Why is that?

It's not very strange once you think about it. The motivation of love automatically shifts your concern from your own safety to the welfare of others. This means that whatever risk is involved in obeying God is set within the larger context of how God will use your obedience for the aid of other people. If your love is activated toward them, then courage is the result!

When you are gripped by the needs of others, it becomes the most natural thing in the world to be alert, to be determined, and to be brave and strong. Your mission becomes larger than your fears. This is your destiny.

God, go ahead and shift my motivation from protecting myself to helping others. Now show me who You want me to help today.

day 53

"Courage, it's me. Don't be afraid." Peter, suddenly bold, said, "Master, if it's really you, call me to come to you on the water." He said, "Come ahead."
Matthew 14:27–29 MSG

Boldness Looks Beyond the Natural

Peter was a fool, wasn't he. Foolish enough to be the only person (besides Jesus) to walk on water. Not bad, huh?

It isn't that Peter suddenly forgot the laws of physics. He lived his entire life on the water; he was very clear that people don't walk on it. But something happened in that amazing moment, and Peter's perspective swung 180 degrees. He went from sheer terror to sudden boldness in an instant. Why?

Because he got a glimpse of a law higher than physics. He saw past the natural realm to the supernatural and realized that this was the world Jesus lived in. And so must he! It was quite an awakening, and for a moment Peter stepped out of his boat and into the realm of the Kingdom. And over time, Peter began to live there consistently.

I want to live there too, God. I don't want my life defined by this natural world but by Your Kingdom reality. Call me out of my boat.

day 54

When they saw the courage of Peter and John and realized that they were unschooled, ordinary men, they were astonished and they took note that these men had been with Jesus.
Acts 4:13 NIV

Company Is Everything

True courage is unusual. It isn't normal. It tends to surprise people—people who wish they, too, were courageous but usually aren't. There is something in human hearts that rises with admiration and longing when they view this kind of courage. This is why people watch a movie like *Braveheart*—they wish they could be like William Wallace, *Braveheart*'s hero. And so they can, in the ways that matter.

Company is everything. The strength of Wallace's convictions brought out the best in the men who followed him. They became braver and more resolute as a result. Peter and John were "ordinary" men with extraordinary boldness—because they lived in the company of Jesus, and that made all the difference! You live in His company too, and that is the source of strength in your life.

God, thank You that You never leave me, never abandon me. If You are with me, then I can be strong and bold in the mission You give me.

day
55

Be strong and courageous, do not fear or be dismayed because of the king of Assyria nor because of all the horde that is with him; for the one with us is greater than the one with him.
2 Chronicles 32:7 NASB

Courage Comes from 20/20 Vision

King Hezekiah, the one who spoke these words, had courageously restored the worship of the true God in Judah after his father's wickedness. He also had the guts to challenge the oppression of Assyria that had assaulted their country for some time.

When the king of Assyria heard that Hezekiah was actually going to resist his invasion, he couldn't believe his ears. *Who is this little upstart who thinks he can throw off the overwhelming power of our rule?* But it wasn't bravado that motivated Hezekiah; it was a penetrating vision of who God was.

This is the key to breaking intimidation in your life—a clear vision of who God wants to be for you. If that vision is fuzzy, let the Bible be your glasses to give you that clear view of God's goodness and power.

God, restore my vision to 20/20 so I can see You and Your bigness in my life. I will not be in awe of anyone but You.

day 56

Oh, love the LORD, all you His saints! For the LORD preserves the faithful, and fully repays the proud person. Be of good courage, and He shall strengthen your heart, all you who hope in the LORD.
Psalm 31:23–24 NKJV

A Recipe of Hope

Nothing builds courage like a good dose of praise! This was David's secret, and he was willing to share it. David blended declarations with petitions in his worship. He shouted out how awesome were the works and character of God, the amazing things He had done in the past, and then went right into urgent pleas for God's deliverance in his situation. The result was a man whose entire life was marked by tremendous courage.

As you eavesdrop on David's worship in this passage, you hear him give a couple of insights into his own courage. First, God's track record is good; the Rebellion does win out in the end. Second, God rewards courage with strength. So when God sees a faithful heart reaching to be brave in the midst of opposition, God rushes to impart strength. That's quite a promise!

Today I bring my own blend of declaration and petition—
Your faithfulness is unceasing, God, and I need it
today in a fresh way!

One day spent in your house, this beautiful place of worship, beats thousands spent on Greek island beaches.
Psalm 84:10 MSG

Be Done with Lesser Things

Spending some time on the beaches of a Greek island sounds pretty awesome. But how much more awesome is just one moment in the powerful and loving presence of King God? It is a sensory experience like nothing else; there are no comparisons. When the love of God washes over you, you cannot remain the same. You are changed! If it's been a long time since you've felt the clear presence of God, ask Him to be near you now; just sit and let Him love you.

When you go into the house of God, you can expect Him to meet you. Your heavenly Lover is even more eager to make His presence known than you are to feel it. So be all there! Ruthlessly set aside distractions and accusations. Go ahead and do it—He's waiting for you now.

Your presence, God, is all I desire and all I need. Let me feel and know Your love with me from the start of this day to the very end.

day 58

He will give you all you need from day to day if you live for him and make the Kingdom of God your primary concern.
Matthew 6:33 NLT

First Things First

Life can be very confusing. Distractions abound. You can easily feel like a gerbil, spinning furiously on its wheel but not really going anywhere.

Into that conundrum, God speaks with clarity: "Pursue the Rebellion above all other things!" More than your job. More than your friends. More than hobbies or sports or the corporate ladder. The New Rebellion is the real world—everything God values and everything He is doing. All your genuine needs will be met when He is your highest priority. Many people pursue the tangible aspects of their life and give them higher priority than the intangibles of pursuing God.

When your spiritual eyes get ahold of Kingdom vision, then your life comes into vivid focus. Potential opportunities and relationships that puzzled you and dissipated your energy before now emerge in stark clarity.

God, I set my heart to seek Your face as my first priority today. I trust You to provide for every other need in my life!

day
59

The LORD would speak to Moses face to face, as a man speaks with his friend. Then Moses would return to the camp, but his young aide Joshua son of Nun did not leave the tent.
Exodus 33:11 NIV

Addicted to God

There are lots of potential things you can get addicted to, lots of "drugs" that want to consume your attention, your resources, and your very life. Work can be an addiction. Food can be an addiction. Entertainment can be an addiction. But you know what? God can be a holy addiction in your life, and you'll never have to worry about detoxing from that One!

The same Joshua who so courageously led a nation into their promised land was a man addicted. Moses would meet with God in the Tent of Meeting and then leave, but Joshua couldn't. He was captured by the presence of God—it consumed his thoughts, his desires, and his feelings. The New Rebellion agrees on this: God's presence is never meant to be a recreational drug; He wants to be an addiction.

God, I want Your presence to be the one thing I most think of, most dream of, and most spend my time and affections upon.

day 60

Don't we take into ourselves the body, the very life,
of Christ? Because there is one loaf, our many-ness
becomes one-ness—Christ doesn't become
fragmented in us. Rather, we become unified in him.
1 Corinthians 10:16–17 MSG

Real Fellowship

The Communion meal of bread and wine is one of the most mysterious and meaningful components of the Christian life. It represents and in some way facilitates your union with Jesus, your fellowship and partnership with Him. It is a sacred and intimate experience, one to enjoy frequently.

At the heart of this sacrament is the miracle of two becoming one, much the same way that a man and a woman are united into one flesh by marriage. By participating in these symbols of the body and blood of Jesus, you are united into life with Him. And it doesn't stop there! You are also united into life with your Christian brothers and sisters. God's presence will always draw you into intimate fellowship with both God Himself and with one another. And this holy partnership will change the world!

God, I want to live the reality that I believe—that I live in You and You live in me. I live in my Christian friends and they live in me.

A veil covers their hearts. But whenever anyone turns to the Lord, the veil is taken away . . . And we, who with unveiled faces all reflect the Lord's glory, are being transformed into his likeness.
2 Corinthians 3:15–16, 18 NIV

day 61

Breaking the Barrier

There is a barrier between people and the presence of God; that barrier is sin. Before you submit your life to God, that barrier veils your ability to see God or understand His ways. But when God moves on the human heart to surrender its will, the barrier is broken and the veil removed.

What seemed like nonsense before now moves into striking clarity. The foolishness of the Cross now comes into sharp relief as the great wisdom of God. With that hindrance removed from your understanding, you can now see Kingdom realities and take your place as a world-changer.

God's presence that was so elusive before now becomes the very oxygen your soul craves. More than that, you become a mirror to reflect the presence of God to all those around you. Are you ready to break the barrier?

Thank You, God, for tearing down the veil of separation. Let my life mirror Your presence to every person in my sphere of influence.

day 62

Give to the LORD the glory due His name; bring an offering, and come before Him. Oh, worship the LORD in the beauty of holiness! Tremble before Him, all the earth.
1 Chronicles 16:29–30 NKJV

Be Afraid . . . Be Very Afraid

Perhaps you've been puzzled by the Bible's periodic reference to the "fear of the Lord" or to "trembling before Him." Why would God want people to be afraid of Him?

Have you ever stood outside in the middle of a hurricane? To feel the force of that power is to feel both an intense admiration and an intense fear. The power of a hurricane is but a dim shadow of the power of God. A peek at the power of His presence should rightly inspire a wonderful—and terrible—awe. But the substantial difference in this comparison is that a hurricane's power is destructive, and God's power is directed by His goodness.

Those who love God know that they are always safe with Him. But that doesn't remove the "trembling" of holy respect that His presence inspires.

God, show me what it really means to fear You in a way that does not put off but rather draws close in intimacy.

These will pay the penalty of everlasting destruction, away from the Lord's presence and from His glorious strength.
2 Thessalonians 1:9 HCSB

A Vacuum of Absence

The Creation not only depended upon the spoken word of God to take original form; it also depends upon His power to sustain its every moment. Scientists still cannot explain why protons cling together at the core of every atom when "like charges" repel—the only explanation is God!

Human history pivots around the central issue of God's presence. Some seek it and find beauty beyond imagination. Others reject it, only to find that its absence becomes their worst nightmare. In fact, hell itself is the fulfillment of people's wish to be free from God.

But the absence of God is the manifestation of every evil thing. There is no accounting for the choice to reject God except for the veil previously discussed. Your mission, should you choose to accept it, is to reveal the winsome beauty of God's good presence.

God, I want to be forever marked by Your contagious presence and by Your "glorious strength." Let it draw many seekers to Your heart.

day 64

[I pray that] you, being rooted and firmly established in love, may be able to comprehend with all the saints what is the breadth and width, height and depth, and to know the Messiah's love that surpasses knowledge, so you may be filled with all the fullness of God. Ephesians 3:17–19 HCSB

Big House

How big is God's love? Big enough that the pursuit of it requires a lifetime.

Your understanding of the character and extent of God's extraordinary love can grow every day of your existence and still have room for the exponential growth of eternity. Now that boggles the mind! Fortunately, God's love is not so much a matter of the mind as it is a matter of the heart. And the New Rebellion hinges upon the hearts of men and women being captivated by this infinite love. But your heart needs some stretching first.

God is vitally interested in stretching your concept of His love. It's a love that is strong enough to root you and secure you in all the uncertainties of life. It's a love that far surpasses your grandest conception of how good God is. And it's a love that will turn your world upside down with transforming power!

Okay, stretch my mind, God. Blow down the doors of my imagination so I can get a bigger glimpse of the vastness of Your affection for me.

If I could speak in any language in heaven or on earth but didn't love others, I would only be making meaningless noise like a loud gong or a clanging cymbal.
1 Corinthians 13:1 NLT

day
65

The Prime Directive

Love is the be-all and end-all when it comes to understanding God. He created you in love. He sent His Son to show you what love looks like. And He will toss away the universe like an empty toilet paper roll one day because He's tired of having to convey His love from afar. He is determined to bring His love up close and personal!

In the meantime He wants you to show that same kind of crazy love to the rest of the world: an intoxicated, go-to-any-lengths, never-give-up kind of love. What do you think—can you go for that?

Thinking about becoming the primo preacher of the world? A worker of miracles? Another Mother Teresa or modern-day martyr? If it doesn't begin and end with love, don't bother! Love is the only currency that flies in the New Rebellion.

I'll be honest, God. Love doesn't always come easily. But I want to love and I choose to love big, just as You do.

day 66

Love is patient, love is kind. It does not envy, it does not boast, it is not proud. It is not rude, it is not self-seeking, it is not easily angered, it keeps no record of wrongs.
1 Corinthians 13:4–5 NIV

Standard Operating Procedures

Learn to love God and love people—that's as fundamental as it gets in the Rebellion. There is no other measure of success than that of love. But what is love? It has to be more than just "Don't worry, be happy"; it has to be more than just warm, mushy feelings or vibrations for world peace.

Fortunately, God spelled it out pretty clearly in this passage from the "Love Chapter." Can you be patient in the midst of extreme and continuous aggravation? Can you return kindness when someone has cut you off in traffic and given you the one-fingered salute? There are tougher tests, aren't there? Someone spreads lies about you, perhaps, or a drunk driver takes the life of someone you love.

The world is looking for supernatural love, a love that defies any logical explanation. Hopefully they will find it in you.

You know me completely, God. If people are going to find this kind of love in me, it's got to come from You. Live Your life through me.

day 67

Trust steadily in God, hope unswervingly, love extravagantly. And the best of the three is love.
1 Corinthians 13:13 MSG

Love Ridiculously!

The Love Chapter ends with a crescendo of passionate commission. With these words, Paul catapults you out into the world armed with the core motivations to change your world for the Kingdom. In fact, these issues of trust, hope, and love are the seeds of God's Kingdom Rebellion. If your journey through life is all about learning to be a son or a daughter of the Kingdom—and it is—then there is no greater assignment than this!

Trust will give you the courage to steadily and faithfully obey God, even when your mind is conflicted. Hope will hold you to the course when your emotions are telling you to jump ship. But extravagant love? Nothing can touch that. And nothing will reconcile people to God like it. There's a love-drought going on, and you've got the water.

Yes, I'm willing to be ridiculous. I'm ready to boggle people's minds with my determination to love continuously and extravagantly.

day 68

Her sins, which are many, have been forgiven, for she loved much; but he who is forgiven little, loves little. Luke 7:47 NASB

Turnabout Is Fair Play

Jesus offered lots of extreme comparisons. Stuff like "The first will be last." Or "He who loses his life will find it." Here, Jesus works another strange paradox: The more you've been forgiven, the more you are able to love. How does that work?

Forgiveness is a powerful thing—a dynamic people intuitively know is not of this world. You've heard the quote "To err is human, to forgive divine," and it's very true. Forgiveness does not spring from the human condition; rather, it flows out of the divine image.

In short, forgiveness flows out of love and elicits love in return. Love that overlooks a debt or an offense creates an actual love-debt. What does this mean for you? Two things: Return the gift of forgiveness with great love. And demonstrate your love by being quick to forgive.

Drive the anchor of love deep into my heart, God. Give me that divine grace to forgive easily and quickly, no matter the offense.

day 69

A new commandment I give to you, that you love one another; as I have loved you, that you also love one another. By this all will know that you are My disciples, if you have love for one another.
John 13:34–35 NKJV

The Litmus Test

What does the world think of when they think about the Christian church? Are they mystified by the irrational love they encounter? Are they amazed? Intrigued? Drawn to try to comprehend this supernatural, selfless love that has no parallel in the non-Christian world?

To be sure, this dynamic does indeed occur at unheralded times and places where God's love is flowing well. And when it does, people's hearts are captivated! At other times, the world sees the opposite: church schisms, moral failures, political anger, power plays . . . you know the drill.

But don't lose heart! Don't give up on Jesus' dream! The New Rebellion seeks the road of humility over arrogance, serving over ruling, love over selfishness. You can't do it without divine grace, but that grace is available to you today.

Oh, make me an uncluttered channel of Your divine love this day, my God. And let people's hearts be touched by it and drawn to You.

day 70

Be completely humble and gentle; be patient, bearing with one another in love.
Ephesians 4:2 NIV

Put Up or Shut Up

The life of the Spirit runs counter to everything that arises naturally in the pre-redeemed human heart. Fortunately, that old heart that used to rule you and define you has been put to death, and in its place has arisen a brand-new you. A heavenly you. And the old impatient, self-seeking, abrasive "you" doesn't rule anymore! God rules.

This is why Galatians says, "Live by the Spirit, and you will not gratify the desires of the sinful nature" (5:16 NIV). If you are going to carry the name of Jesus, then let the Holy Spirit operate in you, showing Himself uniquely in the quality of your love for others. A love that doesn't push its weight around or demand its own way. A love that really seeks the best for other folks.

God, I don't want to talk the talk and not walk the walk. Empower me to care about the people in my life and serve them well.

day
71

Enoch walked steadily with God. And then one day
he was simply gone: God took him.
Genesis 5:24 MSG

Talk About Intimacy!

Every Christ-follower lives simultaneously within two different realms—the spiritual realm of God's Kingdom and the natural realm of this earth. Both are vital to God's interests, but one realm is eternal while the other is temporary. In one realm, the will of God is lived out exclusively, while the other realm is a battleground of wills, the venue of the New Rebellion.

Intimacy with God is about learning the motivations and values and purposes of the Kingdom realm and living those things out here on earth. It's a heavenly relationship that affects every earthly relationship with heavenly life.

Enoch was an amazing guy. There's not much written about him, but the implication is that he became so comfortable in the Kingdom realm that, perhaps without even realizing it, he simply shifted over into heaven itself. Not bad!

God, I want to live in full agreement with and connection to Your Kingdom. Lead me into that kind of intimacy with You.

day 72

You are no longer a slave, but a son; and if a son, then an heir through God.
Galatians 4:7 HCSB

Progression #1: Children

God's story of restoration begins in the Garden of Eden when intimacy was stolen away by sin and God began the long journey back. The original intimacy between God and His creation was so complete, and the loss of it so devastatingly thorough, that renewal came at a very high price. But that price was paid.

The door is now open and access has been restored, but the stages on the return trip come slowly to those who were born into separation. Stage one is huge: no longer a slave, but a son. Talk about an upgrade!

Throw off the old slave mentality of a sinner just barely saved by God's begrudging grace. Far from that, you are a son! Dearly loved and diligently sought. You have been ransomed and released from your captivation. Intimacy is your birthright; it belongs to you.

God, You are my true Father, and I am Your true child. Nothing and nobody can take that away from me now. I belong to You.

day 73

I no longer call you servants, because a servant does not know his master's business. Instead, I have called you friends, for everything that I learned from my Father I have made known to you.
John 15:15 NIV

Progression #2: Friends

Being a son or a daughter of King God is the thrill of a lifetime. You are owned and you have ownership in His Kingdom. But that's not enough for God; He wants more! And so He calls you to the next stage of intimacy: friendship.

It's a natural progression, really. When a son or a daughter grows up, the relationship changes with the parents. The intimacy is no longer shaped primarily by submission and obedience but by a growing friendship—a capacity to share life with a sense of equal partnership. How could that possibly apply to you and God?

It is beyond understanding, but not beyond experience. Inexplicably, He invites you to that place of true fellowship and partnership. It is a gift beyond measure, and not everyone can receive the gift. Will you?

God, I humble my heart to receive Your mind-bending invitation to deeper intimacy with You. I come trusting and won't hold back.

day 74

As the Scriptures say, "A man leaves his father and mother and is joined to his wife, and the two are united into one." This is a great mystery, but it is an illustration of the way Christ and the church are one.
Ephesians 5:31–32 NLT

Progression #3: Lovers

Intimacy is a scary thing. There's no hiding, no pretending in intimacy. That level of emotional nakedness is intimidating, to say the least. But it is also blissful beyond imagination. Sort of like the anxious thrill of marriage.

Stage one was an enormous leap from slave to child of God. Stage two was an unprecedented invitation to partnership and friendship. But stage three will blow you away! Eden restored means an absolute departure from your old, self-contained identity and a merger into oneness with God Himself. The only analogy that even comes close is marriage.

Are you willing to go there? To approach a singleness of mind, a oneness of heart, a unity of spirit with your Lord, your Creator? It's what you were made for; yes, it's actually your heart's true home.

God, I don't feel ready, but I know I was crafted for this one purpose: to know You and live with You in the joy of intimacy.

Simeon . . . was righteous and devout, looking for the consolation of Israel; and the Holy Spirit was upon him . . . And there was a prophetess, Anna . . . a widow to the age of eighty-four. She never left the temple, serving night and day with fastings and prayers.
Luke 2:25, 36–37 NASB

New Rebellion Icons

Where does one find a road map to intimacy? How many have gone there and can help you do the same? Perhaps you know someone farther down the road than you, someone who would encourage you and point the way. Some examples can even be found in the pages of the Bible.

Simeon and Anna were two intimate souls who devoted their lives to the New Rebellion. Their hearts cared deeply about the condition of God's people—which shows that their interests were bound up in the interests of God. How do you know how to find the interests of God? It's simple: You spend time with Him.

Prayer and fasting open a window into His heart. God's Word illuminates His heart. His Spirit activates your heart. It's a lifelong journey, but the invitation is yours.

God, I'm just an ordinary person, but You promise to lead me into an extraordinary life of intimacy. This is one invitation I'm accepting!

day 76

The LORD passed by, and a great and strong wind tore
into the mountains and broke the rocks in pieces
before the LORD, but the LORD was not in
the wind; and after the wind an earthquake
. . . and after the earthquake a fire . . .
and after the fire a still small voice.
1 Kings 19:11–12 NKJV

Kything: A Soul Connection

When a couple has been married for years, a funny thing starts to happen—they learn to read each other's mind! One person will start a sentence, and the other will finish it. He will open his mouth to ask for the sugar, but it's already in motion. She will be thinking about something, and he will start talking about it. The term for this kind of wordless communication is *kything*.

This evidence of natural intimacy carries over into spiritual intimacy. When your heart is tuned to God's "wavelength," you'll pick up what's on His heart. As a result, you'll know how to pray, how to serve, and how to speak.

God gave Elijah a multiple-choice question: Where is My voice? Is it in (a) the tornado, (b) the earthquake, (c) the fire, or (d) the whisper? It was a lesson in kything and another step toward intimacy.

Teach me to listen, not just to Your words, but to Your heart, God. I desire to know You as deeply as possible on planet Earth.

day
77

He who dwells in the shelter of the Most High will
rest in the shadow of the Almighty.
Psalm 91:1 NIV

Chill 'n' Hang

This world is so task-oriented and relationally challenged that intimacy requires some remedial education. It's easy to get taken with the concept of intimacy and want to rush off and get busy doing it. But intimacy isn't a task to be checked off your list so you can get on with the Rebellion. Intimacy is a new way of thinking and a new way of living that encompasses all of life and undergirds the Rebellion.

The psalm writer here had a real revelation of that in this simple lyric. "Dwelling" and "resting" are key ingredients to intimacy. To dwell with God means to live with God—to simply hang out and be with Him. Resting means to chill out from all the activity that engulfs your soul, even religious activity. These skills don't come easily, but they are essential to an intimate life.

I'm starting to get it, God. Still all the noise in my head and my compulsive activity. Teach me how to chill and hang out with You.

day 78

In the beginning the Word already existed.
He was with God, and he was God.
John 1:1 NLT

The Old Word Is the New Word

Sara Groves has a song called "The Old Word Is the New Word." In it, she sings about how the ancient words of God are as alive and vibrant and relevant today as they ever were. Somehow, God's Word never wears out or gets out of date.

Out of the millions of words God has communicated to His people over the years, one word stands out. It is *the* Word, Jesus Himself. Hebrews 1:1–2 says, "In the past God spoke to our forefathers through the prophets at many times and in various ways, but in these last days he has spoken to us by his Son" (NIV).

God didn't just speak through His Son, He spoke in His Son. Jesus was, in His very character and life, a living book to declare the heart of God to a needy world.

God, I'm listening. I want the Word of Your life to speak loudly through the book of my life. Help me look like You.

day
79

Your word I have hidden in my heart,
that I might not sin against You.
Psalm 119:11 NKJV

Your 3,000-Mile Tune-Up

Your soul is a delicate instrument, capable of navigating the intricate pathways of thought and relationship. The more delicate an instrument, the more maintenance it needs to run at its optimum, and the soul is no exception.

In a similar way to which a mechanic hooks your car up to a diagnostic computer for regular maintenance, so God's Spirit diagnoses your soul through the Word, highlighting areas that need attention or repair. What condition is your soul in? Is it neglected or well maintained?

Wise men and women learn to store up God's Word inside them, so that there is a constant renewal taking place—sin confessed, the conscience cleansed, the heart restored, and the mind equipped. A well-tuned soul is a potent force for changing the world, and changing the world is what the New Rebellion is all about.

Search me and know me, God. Shine the light of Your Word all through me—I trust Your gentle management of my heart.

day 80

I meditate on your precepts and consider your ways. I delight in your decrees; I will not neglect your word.
Psalm 119:15–16 NIV

Twenty-Four/Seven

Here's another analogy: Regular meditation on God's Word functions like a background virus check that continuously scans your soul for intruders. A condemning voice, a lie about God, a vague discouragement, a subtle temptation . . . these are just a few of the "viruses" that the Bible has the power to uncover and eliminate.

How do you meditate on God's Word? You read it; you ponder it. You put yourself inside it and see how it fits. You let your imagination run over what the Author was thinking when He wrote it. Then you get still and listen to the Spirit's comments and convictions. It's a very relational, intimate experience.

When you hang out in the Bible, you'll find your spiritual sense sharpened—your mind becomes more keen, your emotions more alive. Frankly, you'll experience God more vividly and powerfully in your life.

Okay, God, lay me open like a book and read the pages of my life. I won't neglect what You have spoken.

day
81

Every word of God proves true, He defends all who come to him for protection. Do not add to his words, or he may rebuke you, and you will be found a liar.
Proverbs 30:5–6 NLT

Absolute and Absolutely Trustworthy

True perspective on the Word of God—as well as the God of the Word—arises out of a specific character quality: humility.

Without humility, neither God nor His words can be rightly understood. Humility is not thinking badly of yourself; it is not poor self-image. Rather, humility is an accurate image of self and of God. Humility recognizes the vastness of wisdom and strength and goodness that is contained in God and then bows in worship before Him.

This is the only posture from which God's words can be honored and obeyed with faith. And faith, combined with patience, releases the inherent power of those words to accomplish their intended purpose. "Imitate those who through faith and patience inherit the promises" (Hebrews 6:12 NKJV). Those who trust that God's words are absolutely bombproof will unlock God's promises.

God, I bring my life under the authority of Your words.
I will not confuse them or dilute them with my
own limited understanding.

day 82

So is my word that goes out from my mouth: It will not return to me empty, but will accomplish what I desire and achieve the purpose for which I sent it.
Isaiah 55:11 NIV

The Last Word

God always gets the last word. Come to think of it, He had the first word, too! His words (see Genesis 1) formed matter out of creative thought on an artistic scale beyond comprehension: planets, microbes, black holes, and you. Each word of God contained an explosive power to accomplish exactly what was in His mind. And guess what? Nothing's changed.

Every word of God continues to carry with it divine power to create purpose, to redeem failure, and to oppose the works of Satan. And so it will be in your life. This is not fatalism! In today's pop theology, it's common to hear, "It will all work out." But it's God's purposes that will stand. Yes, evil has its season, but the heart of God, expressed through the words of God, will outlast evil and destroy evil.

God, I trust the divine power and good intent of all Your words in my life. I'm confident that You have a fantastic future in store for me.

Let the word of Christ richly dwell within you, with all wisdom teaching and admonishing one another with psalms and hymns and spiritual songs, singing with thankfulness in your hearts to God.
Colossians 3:16 NASB

day
83

Cull Your Collection

You know how your CD collection can age? Every decade or so, it's not uncommon to find that your tastes have changed and that you're not listening to the same songs and groups anymore. So what are the songs that fire your imagination these days, that fill your heart?

It's not just the tunes, but it's the messages as well. Do the messages contain God's wisdom? Do they reinforce God's passions? Do they encourage you in your pursuit of Him? Paul's advice is to let the words of Jesus percolate inside you—to live there, to ruminate, to interact, and ultimately to change you.

Let the melody of truth bubble up and spill out of you in songs of praise. Tell anyone who will listen all the fantastic things God has done and who He is. Let your heart touch His with intimate songs of adoration and affection.

I cherish Your words, God, the ones that join my heart with Yours and the ones that express my deepest thoughts and desires.

day 84

All Scripture is inspired by God and is profitable for teaching, for rebuking, for correcting, for training in righteousness, so that the man of God may be complete, equipped for every good work.
2 Timothy 3:16–17 HCSB

Food to Get Well-Rounded

A well-balanced diet is essential for healthy living. Natural foods have a mysterious way of imparting good nutrients your body needs as well as strengthening your immune system to resist the things that want to attack your body.

Your spiritual "body" operates in much the same way: The presence of God in His words brings the ingredients for spiritual health. Words of wisdom, words of illumination, words of direction—they equip you and impart the courage and discernment to be a Rebel for God. At the same time, His words challenge your incorrect views of reality; they highlight destructive behavior and bring correction to places that are misguided.

Whatever situation you are facing in your journey today, you can know without doubt that these words of God are truly inspired. They are God-breathed expressions of His heart for you.

God, I want You to know that I'm grateful for the gift of Your words and that I receive them into my soul for health and growth today.

day 85

Hearing this, Jesus was amazed and said to those following Him, "I assure you: I have not found anyone in Israel with so great a faith!"
Matthew 8:10 HCSB

Says Who?

What could Jesus have possibly heard that would elicit such praise? In short, Jesus heard a man who understood authority and, beyond understanding it, recognized it when he saw it. This man was a Roman commander, responsible for about a hundred soldiers. When Jesus offered to heal his dying servant, the commander told Jesus just to speak the word—he knew it would be accomplished immediately because of Jesus' authority.

There is only one other reference in the Bible to Jesus' being amazed, and it also had to do with faith—in this case, the lack of it. In His hometown, Jesus found that people kept Him in the old box of carpenter and, amazingly, would not recognize His new authority. Thus, no miracles. A revelation of Jesus' authority in your life will unlock the power of God for miracles!

God, let my heart become deeply convinced of Your authority in my life and my world. I want to host Your miracle power this day.

day 86

Then the woman came back to Jesus, went to her knees, and begged. "Master, help me."
Matthew 15:25 MSG

Online Access

For the second time Jesus commends the faith of a non-Jew. Though He was uniquely sent to bring good news to Israelites, Jesus was frequently stymied by the Jews' preconceived ideas of what they thought Messiah would be. But it was a Canaanite woman in this case who had desperate faith for her daughter's deliverance from a demon.

Strangely, Jesus did not make it easy for her. First He ignored her, then He told her that miracles were reserved for Jews, and finally, He gave her an outright insult. But far from being hard-hearted, Jesus was merely setting the stage for her extraordinary faith. He intentionally placed a few obstacles in her path in order to see whether she would cross them. And cross them she did.

What about you? Can your faith cross obstacles in order to believe God?

God, my trust is not in my own faith but in
Your character. Knowing You cannot fail me,
I will cross any obstacle to believe You!

This is why the promise is by faith, so that it may be according to grace, to guarantee it to all the descendants—not only to those who are of the law, but also to those who are of Abraham's faith.
Romans 4:16 HCSB

day 87

Abraham Rocks!

God's promise of redemption and restoration has always been based upon grace. In other words, people have never been capable of earning it; it has always been a gift based upon the kindness of God. This was true in Abraham's day, and it's true in this day. But grace is not automatic—it does not flow indiscriminately to all. It is *a present* offered to all, but one that can be unwrapped only by faith.

And this is why Abraham rocks. Because he didn't have Paul there to explain it to him. He didn't have Paul or Jesus or anyone else. He simply knew God was offering him a promise and a future that he could never obtain by his own effort. He could own it only by faith, by relinquishing his inability for God's ability. The New Rebellion is built upon this same quality of faith.

I know I can't gain any of Your promises, God, by my own effort. So I choose to trust You, Your faithfulness, and Your ability in my life.

day 88

We are always confident, knowing that while we are at home in the body we are absent from the Lord. For we walk by faith, not by sight.
2 Corinthians 5:6–7 NKJV

Close Your Eyes with Confidence

Have you ever played that game where you close your eyes and fall backward into the arms of your friends? Sometimes it's part of a ropes course. But no matter where it is, it's very, very difficult. Every instinct for self-preservation tells you that you don't fall into something you can't see. It just doesn't make sense. But this is precisely the way faith works!

Faith is like radar—it's a virtual set of eyes that functions in a realm beyond sight. Faith is your eyes to "see" what God's up to in the Rebellion. These eyes allow you to perceive the presence of Jesus, the will of the Father, and the wisdom of the Spirit. You can't see them, but they are exceedingly real and bring confidence to walk your spiritual journey well.

Give me confidence, God, to trust the things I can't see with my eyes but know are true by faith.

day
89

The only thing that counts is faith expressing itself through love.
Galatians 5:6 NIV

Real Faith Looks Like Love

Talk about a blanket statement! Could Paul really mean it? The only thing that counts in the Kingdom culture, in the spiritual realm of God, in heaven itself . . . the only thing that has abiding value is that your heart be motivated by faith in God, which in turn produces loving behavior. Wow! It's simple but profound.

If you're honest, there are a lot of potential motivations in life. One of the most common is fear. What about pride? Or greed? Those three spawn most of what you see on the news, not to mention a good bit of what creeps into your own heart. In contrast, God invites you to do everything in your day out of an unshakable trust in Him. The freedom that emerges from that trust will empower you to love every person you know, and even those you don't.

This is the intention of my day: to trust and to love. To love God, to love myself, and to love my neighbor. Help me, God.

day 90

Whatever is not from faith is sin.
Romans 14:23 NKJV

Only One Motivation Counts

Yes, this declaration is in your face. But it is also clear and true and, ultimately, liberating.

If you see this statement as a grim-faced indictment of your spirituality, then you're looking at it wrong. Think about it this way: The only dynamic in this world that can capture you and make you its slave is sin, in one form or another. Sin is the enemy of God and is your enemy, too. Sin is what deceives you and lures you into a net of unhappiness and alienation. But faith is the antidote! The escape.

Faith is your compass to avoid the pitfalls of sin. When you're trusting God, enjoying His presence, and using the wisdom of His words in your life, then you're going to live as a free man or woman. And this is the hope of every Rebel.

Thank You for giving me the gift of faith, God.
With Your help, I will cherish that gift and
avoid the entanglements of sin today.

day 91

I didn't want some petty, inferior brand of righteousness that comes from keeping a list of rules when I could get the robust kind that comes from trusting Christ—God's righteousness.
Philippians 3:9 MSG

Don't Go Generic—Choose Name-Brand!

Of course this passage is speaking tongue-in-cheek by describing any brand of righteousness that comes from human effort. Like Internet offers in spam e-mail, you can't always trust the promises of off-brand merchandise. And when it comes to self-righteousness, you can treat that the way you would a get-rich-quick scheme! It's not going to happen. Anyone who takes the bait is a schmo.

So Paul declares that he didn't get suckered into the world's scheme of pseudo-righteousness when he had an offer of authentic, bulletproof righteousness from God Himself. And it's free on top of that!

But it's not always as obvious as this, is it? This culture is hard-wired to a performance mentality exemplified by personal effort and not by faith. So it takes heart revelation to accept the work of Jesus and stop trying to earn God's favor.

God, I'm done trying to keep all the rules of what I think is a righteous life. You're my only source of goodness and I trust You!

day
92

We have different gifts, according to the grace given us.
Romans 12:6 NIV

Gift-Wrapping Included

God has wrapped up an amazing set of abilities inside your skin! Ever thought about that? The problem comes when the abilities you most want seem to be trapped inside somebody else's skin. And they just won't fit in yours.

This issue really comes right back to the matter of trust: Do you trust the wisdom and generosity of God, who decided what gifts to put in you? When He says, "It is very good" over you, does your heart whisper under its breath, "I beg to differ"?

Your gifts are a manifestation of God's grace in your life. Equipment for the Rebellion. These are the specific strengths and abilities that flow out of you without great effort, and when they do, they bring honor to your Creator and fulfillment to your soul.

God, I'm not going to fight You anymore on this. I accept the abilities You have placed in me with gratitude and trust!

day 93

God's various gifts are handed out everywhere, but they all originate in God's Spirit . . . Each person is given something to do that shows who God is.
1 Corinthians 12:4, 7 MSG

Do Your God Thing

Now that's a cool thought—that your gifts actually show the world something about who God is! What an amazing reality. They come from Him and actually are an expression of Him in you.

So just follow the logical progression. If your spiritual gifts show who God is, then the more you use those gifts, the more God is seen. And this is the commission of the New Rebellion: to showcase the beauty of God and so bring His Kingdom rule more and more to planet Earth. So a big part of your job is just that, to use the special abilities God planted inside you.

This means that when you lead wisely or give generously or serve others without recognition, you are in fact living out the Kingdom of God right then and there. Cool, huh?

Give me the courage, God, to be the real me. To not try to be someone else but to use my spiritual gifts to display Your awesomeness.

day 94

Based on the gift they have received, everyone should use it to serve others, as good managers of the varied grace of God.
1 Peter 4:10 HCSB

Don't Hold Back

Now that you know your gift is an expression of God Himself and comes with a unique grace to operate through you, Peter wants to give you the overarching context for using your gift—use it to serve others.

Your gifts are not primarily about self-fulfillment, although that tends to happen. The core purpose of your spiritual gifts is to reveal God and serve others. So this is a good way to even identify your gifts if you're not sure what they are: Ask yourself how you like to help others. What brand of serving flows out of you most naturally? Is it mercy or is it truth? Is it instruction or leadership? Is it healing or discernment?

Ask those who know you best, or take one of the many spiritual-gift inventories that are available now. Get equipped today!

God, I really want to be motivated to bless and encourage the people You've set into my life; empower the Rebellion today through me.

day
95

Since you are eager to have spiritual gifts, try to excel in gifts that build up the church.
1 Corinthians 14:12 NIV

Pursue the Giver

Try to imagine your coming birthday. You're seated on the family room couch and are surrounded by presents wrapped in every conceivable hue and texture. Friends crowd around expectantly, but you're strangely uninterested. The presents can wait; you'll get to them eventually.

Not hardly! You'd be ripping paper and spitting bows in all directions. You've barely kept your hands off them all day, and now it's time to release your appetite. Which scenario describes your eagerness for the gifts that come from God?

God's gifts outlast, outperform, and outsatisfy anything you'll get on your birthday, so why be passive about these Kingdom deposits? Just as it delights you when your gifts to friends light them up, so it delights the heart of your heavenly Father when you get excited about the gifts He sends you.

God, You know me inside and out, and I can only imagine how lavish Your gifts must be for me. I want everything You've got for my life!

day 96

This salvation, which was first announced by the Lord, was confirmed to us by those who heard him. God also testified to it by signs, wonders and various miracles, and gifts of the Holy Spirit distributed according to his will.
Hebrews 2:3–4 NIV

Shine!

As if spiritual gifts weren't enough already! Now, in addition to all the wisdom and goodness that God has poured into your life through His gifts, He's saying they are a lasting confirmation of your salvation. In other words, they are proof positive that you are a citizen of another realm—a citizen of heaven, of God's Kingdom. Which means, let them shine!

Everyone in this world has natural abilities and gifts, but God's gifts are different: They are supernatural! They stand out. And they are meant to draw attention to God. Do you find it hard to believe that God wants to use your gifts as a sign, as a wonder, perhaps even as a conduit for miracles? Well, believe it! Throughout the Bible, God has constantly evidenced the New Rebellion by miracles, and He's not stopping now.

God, I don't have any power in myself to wake up this world,
but I know that You do. Activate my gifts with
Your supernatural power!

day
97

Kindle afresh the gift of God which is in you
through the laying on of my hands.
2 Timothy 1:6 NASB

Stir the Pot

In Paul's education of Timothy, he makes two important points that also apply to you. First, God's gifts can lie dormant until they are activated by prayer. If you want to see God move through you more powerfully, get godly friends or spiritual leaders to lay hands on you, asking God to release His gifts more fully inside you. God is eager to answer that prayer!

Second, even after your spiritual gifts are active, they can go dormant again due to neglect. Perhaps you feel that God has used you more in the past than He is now. Don't ever think it's too late to move with God again! Paul tells Timothy to stir it up. How do you do that? Just start using those gifts again. He won't take them back; He'll be right there to move through you again.

I don't intend to go through my life carrying unwrapped presents! I will activate, stir up, and release everything You have placed within me, God.

day 98

Yes, there are many parts, but only one body. The eye can never say to the hand, "I don't need you."
1 Corinthians 12:20–21 NLT

Good Connections

When you neglect God's gifts in your life, you believe the lie that you're not important and you ignore your place in the Rebellion. The opposite danger is the temptation to think too highly of yourself and you ignore your need for others' gifts in your life. And it's this potential pitfall that Paul warns about here.

The beauty of God is revealed in the multifaceted dimension of His "body," the Christian community. Every person has a unique and vital role to play—a role that benefits the entire body. But just as a body is interdependent on the function of thousands of parts, so your well-being hinges upon everyone else in your community functioning healthily in their gifts.

This should breed a constant humility as well as the passion to release, not only your own spiritual gifts, but the gifts of others.

God, don't let me arrogantly look down on others whose gifts don't seem that impressive. Show me how

day 99

"Do all that you have in mind," his armor-bearer said.
"Go ahead; I am with you heart and soul."
1 Samuel 14:7 NIV

Heart and Soul

Jonathan, son of King Saul in the Old Testament, had just proposed the ridiculous—that he and his armor-bearer, just the two of them, go attack an outpost of two dozen enemy soldiers! "This is madness" might have been a reasonable reply; instead, this man of courageous vision affirms the power of their community: I am with you. I am committed to you. I believe in you, and together we can do anything.

And they did!

Do you have such a soul mate? Someone who believes in you and in whom you believe? Someone who will walk into any danger in order to protect and defend you, and you him? If you do, then you know the power of community. Sadly, the busyness and ambition of this culture facilitates superficiality and makes true community quite rare. Think about it.

God, I'm beginning to see that community lies at the heart of Kingdom living. Please establish this kind of friendship in my life.

day 100

Just as lotions and fragrance give sensual delight,
a sweet friendship refreshes the soul.
Proverbs 27:9 MSG

Refreshment

If you were asked if you have friends, you would probably be quick to answer, "Yes, of course." Yes, but what is the *quality* of your friendships? Real friends are more than acquaintances, more than people you see regularly, and even more than people you enjoy being around. True friends know your soul and, in a very real sense, live life with you and interpret life with you. The Rebellion requires such community.

This quality of friendship refreshes and renews your heart, a heart that is quickly expended and drained over the course of most days. With all the people and circumstances that "take" in life, it is vital to have one or two or three who "give," who refill the tank of your soul and help you be the world-changer you are meant to be.

God, I want to be this quality of friend to others. Help me to refresh the hearts of all those around me today.

day 101

Wounds from a friend can be trusted,
but an enemy multiplies kisses.
Proverbs 27:6 NIV

Wonderful Wounds

When it comes to friendship, trust is everything.

When you trust the heart of your friend, you can afford to accept his words of correction or criticism. They may hurt and they may seem insensitive, but if you are convinced that your friend is committed to your good, then you can receive and process those wounds as a healing, empowering force in your life. Sometimes the one thing you most need is the one thing you are most reluctant to hear.

On the other hand, people with questionable motives will always say what they think you want to hear, which clouds your judgment of them and fails to address the honest needs of your life. Flattery is a dangerous weapon because it appeals to a person's pride and vanity. It effectively separates the wise from the foolish.

Establish humility in me, God, so I can be teachable
and easily receive the corrections of a friend
without getting defensive.

day 102

A plan in the heart of a man is like deep water,
but a man of understanding draws it out.
Proverbs 20:5 NASB

Deep Water

There is perhaps no better window of illumination into the quality of friendship among Kingdom Rebels than this word picture. The heart is a storehouse for many precious things—hopes, dreams, fears, plans, purposes—the core of your very identity. Do you know your heart? You probably know some of it. But no one knows all of it.

One of the beautiful things about friendship is that a friend possesses the skill to draw out your heart and show you your heart. It's a sacred act, really. King Solomon once said that God has set eternity within the human heart.

The contents of your heart are a vast assortment of eternal deposits from the Kingdom of God. If you refuse the cultural currents of superficiality and choose to go deep in your friendships, you will find yourself more effective in God's Rebellion.

God, use me to draw out the treasures of other people's hearts and bring forth the Kingdom purpose that You have set there.

day 103

Encourage one another and build each other up as you are already doing.
1 Thessalonians 5:11 HCSB

Living Stones

The apostle Peter once said that God's people are like living stones being built up into a spiritual house for God to live in. There are many forces that try to tear you down from day to day—voices of failure or discouragement or criticism. But the potent force of friendship reverses those destructive currents and builds people up through the tool of encouragement.

There are few things as powerful in life as encouragement (or conversely, as paralyzing as discouragement). To encourage others is to impart courage, to speak destiny, to remind them of who they really are—not who their circumstances might say they are. Encouragement releases people from lies they sometimes believe about themselves and gives them courage to keep on keeping on. When that happens, the house is built up and God's Rebellion in the earth is advanced!

Connect me deeply into the lives of others today, God.
Use me to encourage those who are hurting and
build the community of faith.

day
104

*G*reater love has no one than this, than to
lay down one's life for his friends.
John 15:13 NKJV

Blood, Sweat, and Tears

So, would you take a bullet for your friend? Fortunately, not many have to make that choice. But you do have many, many choices to make about whether or not you will lay down your life from day to day, whether you will lay aside your own interests for the interests of another, how much of yourself you will give to serve a friend. And frankly, the decisions to give up time or energy are sometimes tougher than giving up your actual life.

This measure of love is the defining quality in a friendship. It was the quality of Jesus' friendship to you—not just His literal death on the cross but the way He fulfilled His destiny to serve others. And the way He continues to impart His own divine resources into your places of need.

God, thank You for being a true friend to me. Now let Your love pour out of me so I can give myself to others in similar fashion.

day 105

They joined with the other believers and devoted themselves to the apostles' teaching and fellowship, sharing in the Lord's Supper and in prayer . . . And all the believers met together constantly and shared everything they had.
Acts 2:42, 44 NLT

An Apostolic Band

This is the quintessential community that Christians have patterned themselves after for two millennia. The nation of Israel was a reflection of God's intent for community. But Jesus built a more vital community on several levels—a group of seventy, a group of twelve, and a group of three. But it spread and went public in the early church.

Thousands of Christ-followers built a community based upon a common destination, a common affection, and a common trust. Their destination was to continue the apostolic ministry of Jesus and live the Rebellion. Their affection was cultivated in communion, prayer, and fellowship. Their trust was displayed by the vulnerable sharing of their possessions. And this is still God's heart for His community all across the world. This quality of fellowship testifies to the power of heaven come to earth.

God, I will reach for this quality of community in my home, in my church, and in my world. Empower us to change the earth!

day 106

I am in them and You are in Me. May they be made completely one, so the world may know You have sent Me and have loved them as You have loved Me.
John 17:22–23 HCSB

The Vision

What is God's idea for church? Given the hundreds of ways that men and women have answered this over the years, the question is a fair one. Not only fair, but absolutely central to the quest of following Christ.

And Jesus Himself laid out the fundamental vision for church as He prayed for His fledgling community at the conclusion of His ministry on earth. At the heart of this prayer lies the truth that God's church is an extension and continuation of the life of Jesus in this world. That although Jesus Himself will not be visibly present through the coming ages, the essential Kingdom relationship He lived in will be present.

This is the crux! The complete unity of heart, mind, and will that Jesus experienced with the Father—He now invites His disciples to live in that depth of relationship.

God, my heart will settle for nothing less than living in the ever-present reality of Your love and Your life inside me!

He is before all things, and in Him all things hold together. He is also head of the body, the church; and He is the beginning, the firstborn from the dead, so that He Himself will come to have first place in everything.
Colossians 1:17–18 NASB

day 107

The Architect

This may be a radical thought, but Jesus is the architect and director of His church! Not the pastor. Not the elders or deacons or board members. Jesus isn't looking to be a figurehead, but the real, live "head," directing His church! How does that work? In addition to the Bible, Jesus speaks through His Holy Spirit to manage the affairs of *His* body, the church.

He has the wisdom the church needs. *He* has a custom-crafted destiny for every faith community. *He* is the source and the object of all identity, mission, and fellowship that mark each local church. So what does that mean for you? Resist political forces that seek to usurp the place of Christ in the church. Affirm gifted and humble leaders who let Jesus do His job. And set a personal example of God's design in your life.

God, thank You that we are not wandering around on our own trying to do church; You are the director of my life and my community.

day 108

This is the rock on which I will put together my church, a church so expansive with energy that not even the gates of hell will be able to keep it out.
Matthew 16:18 MSG

Not a Fair Fight!

This is Jesus' primary statement on the quality of life that He intends for His church: "expansive with energy," explosive with life and transforming power. So potent with divine intent that the opposition of hell is no contest! It's easy to elevate your concept of hell and begin to feel that the cosmic struggle between kingdoms is a fair fight. But it isn't at all. The authority and rule of heaven will sweep away the bulwarks of hell with a swat when the time is right.

To grasp the vitality of the church, it's essential to understand the "rock" Jesus references in this verse. In response to the question "Who do you say that I am?" Peter answers famously, "You are the Messiah." The fulfillment of God's promise, the envoy of heaven. You are the "Son of the living God!"

God, enlarge my feeble understanding of the vastness of Your goodness and power that operate through Your church.

You are . . . fellow citizens with the saints and members of the household of God, having been built on the foundation of the apostles and prophets, Jesus Christ Himself being the chief cornerstone, in whom the whole building, being fitted together, grows into a holy temple in the Lord.
Ephesians 2:19–21 NKJV

The Blueprints

Jesus envisions the church as a spiritual "building," a building of His design. He is the architect; He draws the blueprints. Apostles and prophets are a foundational force to establish essential truths, vision, and strategy for Jesus' church. Everything built into this structure references the lordship and wisdom of Jesus Himself—it's got to be plumb and level.

And then, wonder of wonders, the church becomes a "temple," a place where Jesus shows up and His presence is experienced. A place where the broken are healed. A place of comfort and encouragement and intimate fellowship. A place that affects the world around it, drawing and restoring people hungry for meaning, hungry for love.

The concept of church as "family" has lost some of its impact, but this is an accurate portrait of the kind of mutual commitment and affection that God intends for His people.

God, build my life and my community into Your blueprint, into Your beautiful plan for what church is meant to be.

day 110

By the grace God has given me, I laid a foundation as an expert builder, and someone else is building on it. But each one should be careful how he builds. For no one can lay any foundation other than the one already laid, which is Jesus Christ.
1 Corinthians 3:10–11 NIV

The Management Team Concept

Church was never intended to be the product of one person's gifting or leadership. Since God designed His people to be interdependent, the church can come into the beauty of God's intention only within a context of teamwork.

You, too, have a role to play in building the church. You may not be a pastor or an elder; you may not have any title whatsoever. But you can still be a builder! Through your own foundational relationship with Jesus, you can bring your unique set of gifts and abilities into your community to serve others. Leadership is serving, and anyone can serve.

Sometimes churches still work under the mind-set of hiring one "professional" to do the work of ministry in a church, but this isn't God's idea.

God, help me to see myself the way You see me—as a builder in Your house, as part of Your team for building a life-giving community.

It was he who gave some to be apostles, some to be prophets, some to be evangelists, and some to be pastors and teachers, to prepare God's people for works of service, so that the body of Christ may be built up.
Ephesians 4:11–12 NIV

day
111

The Management Team

In this passage, Paul spells out what the managing team looks like. These are five avenues of leadership that God intends to converge inside His church for one purpose: to equip and prepare God's people to do the ministry.

These verses offer some crucial perspectives. First, the body of Christ has to be built. A church isn't created by constructing a physical building or by hiring a pastor or even by having lots of members. A body is built when each part of the body finds its proper place and function—when the ear is listening and the eye is seeing, and so forth.

So what's the role of leaders in the church? To equip you. What's your role in the church? To be equipped, and to help equip others. Expect God to use you. Don't enter church as a spectator or a consumer. You're not a benchwarmer; you're a key player!

God, I know You have placed gifts and abilities inside me that are meant to serve others. I'm ready to be a player for You.

day 112

God has put all things under the authority of Christ, and he gave him this authority for the benefit of the church. And the church is his body; it is filled by Christ, who fills everything everywhere with his presence.
Ephesians 1:22–23 NLT

The Ministry Team

People often get disappointed in church. Someone hurts their feelings, their gifts aren't recognized or appreciated, someone lets them down. It has been said that church would be fantastic—if it just weren't for the people. The problem is, of course, that people are flawed creatures and make mistakes. And as long as people are involved, church will be a messy business.

But it's also a holy business. And God still breaks into this humanity with His beauty and awesomeness. The church is His body, and He loves it with a consuming passion! He is committed to using His people to change the world. You can't expect perfection among imperfect people, but you can expect God to show up when you're together. More than that, you can actually be an avenue for His presence!

I will not be put off by the problems I encounter in the church; instead, I will be an agent for healing and serving this body.

I have given them Your word; and the world has hated them, because they are not of the world, even as I am not of the world. I do not ask You to take them out of the world, but to keep them from the evil one. They are not of the world, even as I am not of the world.
John 17:14–16 NASB

day
113

Mission Possible

The task is not an easy one: reconciling men and women with their Creator and Lord. The breach, the offense, is a real one, and the result is a very tangible separation and hostility. Add in Satan's role as Deceiver, Accuser, and Liar, and the drama of human history takes on all the twists and turns of a soap opera. A very serious soap opera.

Knowing the challenges better than any other, Jesus prayed over His disciples on the eve of His departure, communicating to them a defining identity: You are My ambassadors. You will not often be welcomed by people. You will work inside this fallen world, but you will be distinctly different from it. In fact, you will be as much a foreigner here as I, Jesus, have been. But you will be "kept" . . . you will be safeguarded and empowered by My Spirit.

God, I receive this identity for myself: I am sent. I am kept by You. I operate in this world but am not owned by it.

day 114

> Paul stood in the middle of the Areopagus and said, "Men of Athens! I see that you are extremely religious in every respect. For as I was passing through and observing the objects of your worship, I even found an altar on which was inscribed:
> TO AN UNKNOWN GOD."
> Acts 17:22–23 HCSB

Carpe Diem

Relevance means understanding the culture and mind-set of the people you are inviting to know Christ. Relevance means finding creative connections into people's psyches. You're not being manipulative; you're looking for opportunities to communicate effectively and seizing the moment.

Paul did this so well in Athens. Essentially, he just paid attention. And by doing this, he noticed the altar to the unknown god, which became his point of connection. Although the Athenians were steeped in their own mythology, they were also hungry for "reconciliation," if you will, with the divine.

Paul capitalized on this hunger by identifying their felt need for spiritual connection, and then opening a door into God's passion for them through Jesus. Your ability to connect with others for the sake of the Kingdom will depend, not upon your great Bible knowledge, but upon your compassion and creativity.

God, help me to love others as You do and to pay attention to the unspoken cry of their hearts so I can introduce them to You.

day 115

Jesus Christ is the same yesterday
and today and forever.
Hebrews 13:8 NIV

The Message Stays the Same

One of the fears of being relevant to the world is the legitimate concern that the essential message of the gospel may be compromised in the process. Or, in Jesus' language, that you might be not only *in* the world but also unwittingly become *of* the world.

God's message is, and will always be, Jesus Christ. The heart of the Father has been reaching for men and women throughout history to convey the depth of His loving passion for them and to bridge the gap of separation between humanity and heaven. The life and death of Jesus conveyed this redemptive message in exquisite detail.

There is no country, no language, no American subculture where Jesus is not relevant. The challenge—and the opportunity—is to make the connection effectively. And this calls for wisdom. The best way you can become a New Rebel for Jesus is to *know* Him really well!

I want to know You, God, and the vastness of Your love more thoroughly and convincingly every day of my life!

day 116

I didn't take on their way of life. I kept my bearings in Christ—but I entered their world and tried to experience things from their point of view.
1 Corinthians 9:22 MSG

But the Methods Change

Relevance means that the unchanging message of Jesus Christ must be communicated in ways that are constantly changing. Culture is in constant flux in every society—and the more culture changes, the more the methodology of conveying Christ must adapt.

Paul says it eloquently: "I . . . tried to experience things from their point of view"! People are not enemies to be attacked with truth but loved into truth. And people can tell when they are loved. You will never be able to convey a larger body of truth than you are able to love that body of people.

In this generation, the value of relationship exceeds the value placed on truth. And since God values both, this is your opportunity to go broad and deep in your relationships, knowing that God will open up divine opportunities for conveying His truth in authentic ways.

Increase my genuine love for people, God. Help me to never exceed in truth where I am willing to go in relationship.

day
117

You are the salt of the earth. But what good is salt if it has lost its flavor? Can you make it useful again?
Matthew 5:13 NLT

Spice It Up!

Most people are less interested in religion than they are in a great meal. People are hungry for flavor in their lives, both literally and figuratively. The problem arises when folks can't make the connection between intimacy with God and the flavor they seek in their lives, not realizing that the latter depends upon the former.

Authentic spiritual vitality is mouthwatering! When people get around it, their appetite for God is aroused. And this, in a nutshell, is God's recipe for bringing His Kingdom upon the earth. He wants your life to be like salt, awakening the senses and inspiring hunger for the "Bread of Life," for God Himself.

And if your life isn't salty, if it doesn't invite curiosity and arouse people's spiritual appetites, then something is fundamentally broken. Ask yourself whether you're being true to your spiritual identity.

God, I want to live true to who You have made me to be. Let this be evidenced by hunger and thirst from those around my life.

day 118

When the turn came for Esther . . . to go in to the king, she requested nothing but what Hegai the king's eunuch, the custodian of the women, advised. And Esther obtained favor in the sight of all who saw her.
Esther 2:15 NKJV

Adaptation with Wisdom

Esther did not forget who she was—a Hebrew God-worshiper in the courts of a pagan king. But, as they say, timing is everything. And Esther's timing was beautiful as she waited for the perfect moment to reveal herself to the king.

And that's not all. In order to be "relevant" to her audience (the king), Queen Esther learned from the culture she was in, not in a way that compromised her integrity, but for the purpose of making effective connections for God's purpose. Through the king's aide, she wisely studied the values of this foreign environment in order to make herself presentable.

Once she obtained favor, Esther was able to be a spokesperson for the intentions of God and make a way for His miraculous intervention. All because she didn't forget who she was!

God, with Your help I will always remember who I am—a son or daughter of the King—and live true to that calling.

day 119

Pharaoh took his signet ring from his finger and put it on Joseph's finger. He dressed him in robes of fine linen and put a gold chain around his neck. He had him ride in a chariot as his second-in-command, and men shouted before him, "Make way!" Thus he put him in charge of the whole land of Egypt.
Genesis 41:42–43 NIV

Adaptation with Integrity

Joseph . . . the boy of great dreams . . . the boy of his father's favor . . . the boy sold into slavery who watched his destiny shrivel before his eyes. He didn't forget who he was either.

Joseph maintained his integrity even while life handed him blow after unjust blow. Miraculously, he did not become bitter but rather used every adversity as an opportunity to adapt and grow and shine with his own inner light. As a household slave, he rose to the top; in prison, he rose to a position of authority; and finally, he obtained the favor of Pharaoh himself and rose to the number two position in the land.

You can be relevant in your world, no matter whether you find yourself in a "prison" of oppressive circumstances or in the "royalty" of ideal circumstances. Adapt to cultural shifts but retain the integrity of your identity in Christ.

God, I won't allow any circumstance to define me. I know who I am and, with Your grace, I will be relevant in any situation.

day 120

When David had served God's purpose in his own generation, he fell asleep.
Acts 13:36 NIV

Tunnel Vision

Do you believe God has a destiny for you? Does that seem far-fetched? Wishful thinking? Well, believe it. It is true.

Every woman or man of God is born into purpose. Your purpose existed in the mind of God long before your parents came together to create you. And that purpose is reflected in the unique blend of strengths and weaknesses, of spiritual gifts and natural abilities that you now possess.

The apostle Paul looked back hundreds of years to comment on the life of King David and set all of David's failures and successes, his trials and his triumphs, into one snapshot of meaning: He fulfilled his destiny! God had a specific purpose for David's life that reflected God's larger purpose for that generation. And despite significant mistakes, David held true to his purpose. How is yours coming along?

God, make my destiny clear so that I can own it and stay true to it, whatever the obstacles. I want to be tunnel-visioned!

day
121

Where there is no vision, the people are unrestrained.
Proverbs 29:18 NASB

Restrain Yourself

Vision is a powerful force in the life of a man or a woman of destiny. Vision directs, vision focuses, and vision restrains.

Vision is not mystical; it is simply a desired future. God's desired future for you. It is the ability to look ahead with spiritual sight and see who you will be and see some of what you will do to participate in God's Kingdom plan for planet Earth. When this vision is kept front and center, it restrains you from getting involved in activities that would be contrary to that vision or hinder it in any way.

The person with vision has a measuring tool to evaluate every opportunity—does it or does it not advance the cause of Christ in my life and move me toward my destiny? This dynamic effectively shapes men and women to live purposefully in the New Rebellion.

Shape me, God. Give me Your vision for my life so that I can be directed, focused, and restrained to be who I'm meant to be.

day 122

Because of Christ, we have received an inheritance from God, for he chose us from the beginning, and all things happen just as he decided long ago.
Ephesians 1:11 NLT

Old Money

People who grow up with old money are shaped in their identity by the consistent presence of privilege in their lives. Frequently, they innately believe they can truly do anything, and they have the means to accomplish it. It's not a bad picture of the spiritual reality behind your Kingdom inheritance.

You have some seriously old "money" in your account: It's who God says you are, what He envisions for your destiny, and the sum of His resources to enable you to accomplish it. When God talks about your inheritance, it would be prudent to show as much interest as you might have in a large natural inheritance. It will change your life!

Those who understand the limitless resource of their inheritance don't place arbitrary boundaries upon their destiny: "Oh, I could never do that." With God backing the operation, you can be and do everything God intends!

I accept Your good intentions for my life, God. I won't limit my destiny by small thinking but trust You for my future.

day 123

He knows us far better than we know ourselves, knows our pregnant condition, and keeps us present before God. That's why we can be so sure that every detail in our lives of love for God is worked into something good.
Romans 8:27–28 MSG

Destination Redemption

If anything lies at the center of God's heart, it's His redemptive nature. He is a restorer, a rebuilder, a renewer of broken dreams and broken lives. If paradise had not been lost and there was no potent spiritual foe, this facet of God's nature would not be seen. Of course, as it is, there is ever-present opportunity to observe and experience the redemption of God.

It's this certainty of God's nature that equips you with the confidence that God is taking every circumstance you encounter—the good, the bad, and the ugly—and transforming it into an unstoppable force for good in your life. Wow! Is that incredible or what?

God's Spirit really does know you better than you know yourself. He knows that you are expectant with destiny. And so He keeps you centered in the goodness of God.

God, I know that not all my circumstances are good. But I also know that You can, and will, release good things in my life through them.

day 124

I know what I'm doing. I have it all planned out—plans to take care of you, not abandon you, plans to give you the future you hope for.
Jeremiah 29:11 MSG

I Love It When a Plan Comes Together

This is the "sun" around which your destiny orbits—being convinced that God knows what He's doing! If that conviction ever gets lost, your destiny spins off into oblivion like a lost satellite. But this truth has a way of anchoring your heart and exerting a gravitational pull that keeps your God-given future in motion.

He has it all planned out—your abilities, your spouse, your work, your ministry, your passions, your relationships. These things are carefully kept in His heart for you; they cannot be lost or stolen unless you give up on them. There is no mistake that He cannot redeem and restore.

God, and His plans for you, is the entire basis of hope for the future. He has it all planned out, and He'll never quit leading you into your destiny.

Thanks for not abandoning me, God. I'm so glad that You've got my future all figured out, because I could never figure it out myself.

The Son is not able to do anything on His own,
but only what He sees the Father doing. For
whatever the Father does, the Son also
does these things in the same way.
John 5:19 HCSB

day
125

The Path to Destiny

Jesus came to reveal the Father—the love of the Father, the intent of the Kingdom, and the culture of heaven. He modeled the Christian life. In fact, Jesus is the only real Christian who has ever lived. But He invites you into His life, into the reality He lived in. You, too, can know the Father, live in the Father's will, and move redemptively in the earth. Generally speaking, this is the destiny of every Christ-follower.

So, if you want to do the things that Jesus did, you'll need to do it the way Jesus did it. And this is His intention. At the root of all He did lay this fundamental reality: Jesus didn't make His own autonomous decisions. He watched what the Father was doing. He listened to the voice of the Spirit. This heavenly communion will release your destiny, too.

Tune me in, God! I set my heart to say what You're saying and do what You're doing. You hold my destiny.

day 126

The word of the LORD came to me, saying, "The hands of Zerubbabel have laid the foundation of this house, and his hands will finish it. Then you will know that the LORD of hosts has sent me to you. For who has despised the day of small things?" Zechariah 4:8–10 NASB

Small Things Precede Big Things

God does not usually just catapult you directly into the fullness of your destiny. Generally, He equips you little by little, increases your faith by incremental stages, so that you are eventually qualified to step fully into your calling. In the midst of this process, it is easy to get discouraged with the smallness of your labors.

Zerubbabel knew this feeling all too well. As governor of the Israelite colony returning from captivity to reclaim their homeland, the process had been painfully slow. The foundation of the Temple had lain barren for two decades, mocking his destiny. God said, "Don't give up. Don't despise small beginnings. Your destiny still awaits you!" And this is your charge as well—don't quit. Don't look down on unimpressive beginnings, but trust God for your full destiny.

I will trust You with the "small beginnings" of my life, God. You are big enough to finish what You have started in my life.

Then Jesus was filled with the joy of the Holy Spirit and said, "O Father, Lord of heaven and earth, thank you for hiding the truth from those who think themselves so wise and clever, and for revealing it to the childlike."
Luke 10:21 NLT

day 127

Simple Minds

Jesus constantly surprised people, was always doing and saying things that people didn't expect. Because the idea of a Messiah had been ingrained in them for centuries, the Jewish concept of what He should be and do was pretty fixed. Perhaps the most significant way in which Jesus went against the grain of their expectations was His love for humility—it evidenced itself in His personal character as well as in what He looked for in His followers.

Which is why He took such delight that God was revealing Himself to the simple and hiding Himself from the arrogant. Those with proud hearts, especially religious pride, found themselves blinded to the truth of Jesus' person, Jesus' power, and Jesus' teaching. But those who come with trusting, open hearts of children receive the treasures of heaven.

God, let this quality of simple trust and childlike faith define my heart and open my eyes to all that You are today.

day
128

He must increase, but I must decrease.
John 3:30 NKJV

Stepping Out of the Spotlight

John the Baptist survived a massive paradigm shift! He had devoted his life to preaching a message of repentance and holiness, knowing that he was there to prepare the way for the Messiah. And of course, the Messiah came. The Deliverer of Israel showed up in the person of his cousin, and recognizing the grace upon Jesus, John baptized Him and watched the affirmation of God and people blossom upon Him.

John even found his disciples drifting off to follow Jesus, which might have been a little tough emotionally. But the real obstacle for John came in watching Jesus unleash a ministry of healing and compassion, in contrast to John's more in-your-face style. But what sustained John—and will sustain you—was his understanding of this one thing: *Jesus must increase! He must get the attention, not me. He must draw people to Himself, not me.*

God, I want You to get all the attention from my life; I want people to see You in me and be drawn to Your beauty.

Have this attitude in yourselves which was also in Christ Jesus, who, although He existed in the form of God, did not regard equality with God a thing to be grasped, but emptied Himself, taking the form of a bond-servant.
Philippians 2:5–7 NASB

day 129

A Savior Complex?

The term *Savior complex* is applied to people who have the delusion that they are the answer to everyone's problems, which is, of course, an expression of pride and the opposite of humility. What's ironic about this whole phrase is that the real Savior doesn't have a Savior complex. He knows that He is the answer to everyone's problems. But rather than flowing out of a false elevation of Himself, it flows out of a perplexing humility, a humility no one quite understands.

Though He was God, He did not trumpet His divinity; rather, He laid aside some of His divine assets in order to enter planet Earth and become human. This quality of self-surrender must replace your natural inclinations toward self-protection in order to follow Him. Paul challenges everyone to adopt this heavenly attitude.

Empty me, God, of all my tendencies to elevate myself and draw attention to myself. Quite simply, I want to be like You!

day 130

You're blessed when you're at the end of your rope. With less of you there is more of God and his rule.
Matthew 5:3 MSG

Less Is More

It is human nature to seek to be self-sufficient. Particularly in America, this trait has been elevated to a lofty idealism. It's the cowboy persona, the I-don't-need-anything-or-anyone mentality.

But Jesus challenges many American "virtues," and this is one of them. "You're not blessed when you've got it all under control," Jesus says in effect. "You're blessed when you are totally out of your human resources, when all you have left is God. In fact, that's where your life really begins!"

It is unfortunate that people tend to wait to tap God's ways and resources until they have used up all their own. Wisdom comes by making room for more of God up front and by getting out of the way so He can work. God's ways automatically bring the blessings that you want to begin with.

Okay, God, my rope is pretty puny, and I don't want to wait until I'm at the end of it to make room for You in my life.

day 131

By the grace given to me, I tell everyone among you not to think of himself more highly than he should think.
Romans 12:3 HCSB

Shrink Your Head

Pride really springs from fear and insecurity. The sense of not being okay, of lacking love and acceptance, is what prompts people to think of themselves more highly than they ought. Jesus is able to address the issue of humility (through Paul in this case) because He has already taken care of the root issue of security. Can you see that?

It is *because* you are loved, *because* you are completely accepted in the family of God, that you no longer need to try to shore up your image or elevate your appearance.

Insecurity shows up in one of three ways: by elevating yourself, by putting yourself down, or by putting others down. But men and women of God don't think of themselves too highly or too lowly—they know who they are! They relish the security in God that sets them free.

By Your grace, God, I will see myself the way You see me—not trying to elevate myself or tear myself down.

day 132

Human wisdom is so tinny, so impotent, next to the seeming absurdity of God. Human strength can't begin to compete with God's "weakness."
1 Corinthians 1:25 MSG

In the Ring with God

Because the whole concept of God being humble appears so absurd, there is a tendency among the proud to despise the ways of God. The idea of God shrinking Himself to the level of humanity, the idea of Him coming as a servant rather than as a warrior, and, most foolish of all, the idea of God being tortured and put to death without resistance is incomprehensible. It is incomprehensible especially to those who are trying desperately to elevate themselves and be accepted by others.

This is why the humility and simplicity of a child are required to understand and receive the "foolish" wisdom and the "weak" might of God. Truly, there is no human strength or brilliance that can take on God. Those who "get it" embrace their weakness and embrace the Strong One, the Giver of life.

I'm starting to get it, God. Humility lies in acknowledging who You really are, acknowledging who I really am, and delighting in both.

All of you, clothe yourselves with humility toward one another, because, "God opposes the proud but gives grace to the humble." Humble yourselves, therefore, under God's mighty hand, that he may lift you up in due time.
1 Peter 5:5–6 NIV

day
133

A Heavenly Paradox

You don't want to find yourself opposed by God! This is not a happy place to be. But those who buy into this world's agenda of self-advancement will find themselves obstructed and afflicted by God Himself. It's not His judgment but His mercy that provokes such action. This opposition is a wake-up call for you to stop, to realize the futility of such a mission. It is a wake-up call for you to humble yourself.

The culture of heaven usually works backward from this world's culture. Human nature leads you to elevate yourself. God says, "Elevate yourself and I will bring you down." Your mind may say, *If you humble yourself, you're a loser*. God says, "If you humble yourself, I will elevate you. It will be in my time and my way, but I will lift you up and honor you!"

God, I want to be elevated in Your way and in Your time. Not for my honor but Yours. I gladly humble myself before You.

day 134

He called the twelve together, and gave them power and authority over all the demons and to heal diseases.
Luke 9:1 NASB

Delegation

Those whom God establishes in humility He entrusts with His power. As the old saying goes, "Power corrupts, and absolute power corrupts absolutely." Because of this tendency in human nature, God is determined to make it abundantly clear that you do not control His power. At the same time, He is determined to partner with His people and allow you to participate in what He's doing.

God's power is delegated from Him and belongs to Him. However, when you bear His authority with humility, you are unstoppable. His power will flow in and through you, allowing you to bring earthly things into alignment with their heavenly design. This is why God heals the sick and sets people free from demonic oppression—because that is their redeemed nature, their destiny.

God, I am willing for Your power and authority to flow through me. Now purify and qualify my heart to move in partnership with You.

My speech and my preaching were not with persuasive words of human wisdom, but in demonstration of the Spirit and of power, that your faith should not be in the wisdom of men but in the power of God.
1 Corinthians 2:4–5 NKJV

Kingdom Life Requires Kingdom Power

There are those who believe that the Christian faith advances upon the correct exposition of Scripture. Yet while biblical interpretation remains vital, Paul was extremely clear that the Kingdom of God moves forward, not through eloquence but through supernatural power. And Paul's life proved it!

Healings. Deliverances. Miracles. Spiritual confrontations. These were the pillars upon which the Holy Spirit changed the first-century world. And in two thousand years, what has changed? Absolutely nothing! The radical resurrection life of Christ is meant to pour through unlikely human beings like you to have an impact on your world.

Today you can be the channel God chooses to impart healing to broken lives. Listen to His voice and move with bold confidence. People are usually surprised but grateful when you ask to pray for their needs. Big needs, big God.

I am a world-changer! Your supernatural life flows in me, Jesus, and with Your help I will make a difference in my world today.

day 136

This is what the LORD says to Zerubbabel: It is not by force nor by strength, but by my Spirit, says the LORD Almighty. Nothing, not even a mighty mountain, will stand in Zerubbabel's way;
it will flatten out before him!
Zechariah 4:6–7 NLT

Your Muscles Aren't Big Enough!

Once again, God is outlining His Kingdom values. It's not your will that matters but His. It's not your strength that will accomplish God's purposes but His. This isn't an insult; it's just reality. Actually, the whole idea that you would move together with God to bring in His Kingdom rule is a mind-boggling grace! This is revelation number one.

Once that concept really gets traction in your mind, it releases such excitement and vision that the tendency is to move out and try to accomplish God's purposes in your own energy. Revelation number two. Nope, it's not your willpower or gifting that will accomplish His purposes. He will empower you with His Spirit. And when His Spirit is moving through you, absolutely nothing will stand in your way.

God, help me get hold of these truths. I want to see You change my world by Your Spirit moving unhindered through my humility and availability.

day 137

God did not give us a spirit of timidity, but a spirit of power, of love and of self-discipline.
2 Timothy 1:7 NIV

Timidity Busters

Once God establishes that it isn't your power and strength that will drive this Kingdom engine, then He has to enlarge your vision for what He intends to do through you. If you wrap your own limitations around His calling on your life, you will squeeze your destiny into a pitiful pulp.

"God has not called us to do what seems possible, reasonable, or normally attainable," Graham Cooke declares. "We're supposed to be doing what is impossible and outrageous." To really believe this requires God to explode our timidity and cloak us with indefatigable confidence in Him.

This is the spirit God intends us to move in. A spirit of power, His power! A spirit of love, His love for others, His love for redemption. And a spirit of self-control that keeps us fixed on His voice and His will.

Break down the constructs of my own timidity and self-limitation, God! Make me believe that You will work miracles through me.

day 138

You will receive power when the Holy Spirit has come upon you, and you will be My witnesses in Jerusalem, in all Judea and Samaria, and to the ends of the earth.
Acts 1:8 HCSB

Power Ties

A decade or two ago, the rage in the business world was all about wearing a power tie—a bold, confident color that projected an image of competence and control. Jesus offers a better deal: The power tie He provides is a 24/7 broadband connection to the Spirit of God. You can move in boldness and confidence knowing that, even though you are weak, He is always competent and always in control. Really.

One is an image, an illusion. The other is reality. Go ahead—pick which power tie you want!

The cool thing is that God never intends for you to be a world-changer on your own power. In fact, Jesus wouldn't even let His disciples get started on the Great Commission until they had been filled up with His Spirit. And He offers you the same deal.

God, that's one offer I want to take. I want Your power moving in me so that I can be Your man or woman in the earth.

day 139

My grace is sufficient for you, for my power is made perfect in weakness.
2 Corinthians 12:9 NIV

Backward and Upside Down

God's ways are counterintuitive! But they work. God draws near those who fear Him. Elevates the humble. Gives power to the weak. Why does He work in such paradoxes? Probably because the earth is backward and upside down. Because heaven is where things are actually "normal."

The whole essence of partnership requires a sense of need. People partner together because they don't have all the time, resources, or talents needed for an enterprise. If one partner ever loses his need for the other partner, it will probably bring trouble to the partnership.

Given this, your sense of need is one of your greatest assets for working together with God for the Kingdom. His commitment to you is that your need will always receive a portion of His empowering grace that more than covers your need. Pretty good deal, eh?

I know I need You, God, and I embrace my dependency upon You. I look today for the grace that strengthens me with Your power.

day 140

I bow my knees to the Father of our Lord Jesus Christ . . . that He would grant you . . . to be strengthened with might through His Spirit in the inner man, that Christ may dwell in your hearts through faith.
Ephesians 3:14, 16–17 NKJV

Inside Out

Most people try to fix things from the outside in. God's way of fixing things is from the inside out.

When people feel too busy, they usually try to change their schedule. God reaches for people's motivations. When people want to lose weight, they look for a diet. God reaches for people's compulsions. When people want to follow Christ, they are usually led to spiritual disciplines. God reaches for their affections. He's always after the heart!

And it's into the heart that He imparts faith, which in turn brings strength. Strength to stand in difficult places, strength to hold to your convictions, strength to change your world. When your motivations, compulsions, and affections are ruled by God, then He has your heart. And when He has your heart, His Spirit empowers you from the inside out. And your behaviors change.

Have my heart, God. I give it to You, it's Yours.
Change me and strengthen me from the inside out.

I will ask the Father, and he will give you another Counselor to be with you forever—the Spirit of truth. The world cannot accept him, because it neither sees him nor knows him. But you know him, for he lives with you and will be in you.
John 14:16–17 NIV

day 141

The Force

"Remember the Force, Luke," goes the famous quote from the movie *Star Wars*. An undercurrent theme throughout the movie series was the conviction that the mission to save the world depended upon an accurate understanding of and cooperation with "the Force." And although they defined the Force in pantheistic terms, there is a truth here: God does not expect you to be a world-changer without being equipped with a supernatural force—the Counselor, the Spirit of Truth.

God's Spirit came to replace and carry on the work that Jesus Himself began on earth. Jesus' response to His disciples' protests at His leaving was that He would not leave them orphans; He would never abandon them. The Spirit would be their constant connection to God—He would live within them and be a consistent force to counsel, instruct, comfort, and lead them. And you.

Holy Spirit, I welcome You into my life as my Counselor and my Friend. Be my constant companion and guide for my life.

day 142

You are not controlled by your sinful nature. You are controlled by the Spirit if you have the Spirit of God living in you.(And remember that those who do not have the Spirit of Christ living in them are not Christians at all.)
Romans 8:9 NLT

Controlling Force

One of the most counterintuitive aspects to being a Christ-follower is that you must relinquish your control on life. Or more accurately, your *attempts* to control life. No one can really control his circumstances or environment; and without God's Spirit, you can't even control yourself!

Most people spend a huge amount of emotional energy trying to control the pieces of their lives, frustrating themselves and injuring others. That job position has already been filled! The Spirit of God intends to control your life, and as you allow Him that role, you will experience good results time after time: peace, wisdom, protection, direction, joy . . . the list goes on.

You used to be controlled by an inner predisposition toward selfishness and brokenness. But that tyrannical grip is broken by God's Spirit, who now rules you with grace and goodness.

Show me, God, when I step in and try to retake the reins of my life. Help me trust You and gladly yield that role to You!

day 143

God has revealed them to us by the Spirit,
for the Spirit searches everything,
even the deep things of God.
1 Corinthians 2:10 HCSB

Teaching Force

There are two kinds of people in the world: those who *think* they know it all and those who know they don't know it all! The most mature follower of Jesus remains in constant need of the Spirit's instruction. In fact, the more you grow in your spiritual life, the more you will learn, and the more you will realize just how vast is the amount of things you don't know. This brings humility, one of God's favorite qualities of heart.

This places you in a position of dependency that opens the door of opportunity for partnership with God, in this case, God's Spirit. It is His job to reveal the Father's heart to you. And what a job it is! It is His job to unlock the meaning behind the words of Jesus so that your life can take on the shape of His will.

Teach me to hear Your voice consistently and accurately, God, so that I can impact my world for You.

day 144

Walk by the Spirit, and you will not carry out the desire of the flesh. For the flesh sets its desire against the Spirit, and the Spirit against the flesh; for these are in opposition to one another, so that you may not do the things that you please. But if you are led by the Spirit, you are not under the Law.
Galatians 5:16–18 NASB

Warring Force

Relatively few people across the world are born into the horrors of war. But spiritually this is not the case. When men and women are born into the Kingdom of God, they are born into war. No one would choose this, and yet it is a reality.

There is ongoing conflict on planet Earth between God and Satan, between the culture of this world and the culture of heaven, between your flesh and the Spirit of God. How do you engage in this war? By making room for the Spirit within you—room for His thoughts, His initiatives, His attitudes. When you are obedient to Him, the flesh is silenced and you are thrust out into Kingdom purpose. When you obey the flesh and its self-centered desires, the Spirit is silenced and you become a liability rather than a Kingdom asset.

Rule me, God! This day cause me to recognize
Your voice and to make war against the
deceitfulness of my own selfishness.

day 145

Do not be drunk with wine, in which is dissipation; but be filled with the Spirit.
Ephesians 5:18 NKJV

Focusing Force

Most Christians want to live for God and please God, but many of them are largely ineffective in the New Rebellion. Why? Because of dissipation. No, not many get physically drunk, but many do get intoxicated and distracted within their souls.

Dissipation is the opposite of concentration. It means to get spread so thin as to lose effectiveness. Jesus used a story to describe how the seed of God's Word gets choked out by the cares and distractions of life—this is dissipation, and it sidelines many a valuable player in the Kingdom of God.

But it's the Spirit's role to cut off dissipation by focusing your attention and your passion upon the things that really matter! Make Him the center of your affection, and you will find the clarity of purpose that your soul craves.

Guard my heart, God, against the clutter this world throws at me every day. Keep me focused by the power of Your Holy Spirit.

day 146

We ought always to thank God for you, brothers loved by the Lord, because from the beginning God chose you to be saved through the sanctifying work of the Spirit and through belief in the truth.
2 Thessalonians 2:13 NIV

Restoring Force

Salvation is usually understood to be that moment you are introduced to Jesus Christ and ask Him to take the throne of your life. However, this is but the barest beginning of salvation. Salvation is about the complete restoration of your life from brokenness to wholeness, from aimlessness to destiny.

Another key role of God's Spirit is to show you the places in your life where you are being robbed of your destiny and help you recover God's true idea of who you are and what you are meant to do. This is literally being "saved" from the power of sin by the "sanctifying work of the Spirit."

God's Spirit gently shines His light upon a hidden place, introduces truth to counter the lie that has been believed, and then—when met with repentance and faith—activates God's freedom within your soul.

Thank You, God, for setting my heart free from the misdirections of my past. Be the force that restores my soul every day.

As we keep his commands, we live deeply and surely in him, and he lives in us. And this is how we experience his deep and abiding presence in us: by the Spirit he gave us.
1 John 3:24 MSG

day
147

Connecting Force

God never intended us to live out the Christian life merely by following a set of principles. This approach to Christianity breeds the legalism of the Pharisees that Jesus attacked with uncharacteristic fierceness. Instead, the call of Jesus was "Follow *Me*!"

Of course, this amazing relationship with God you are invited into causes you to love His ways and follow His commands. But the progression is important: It isn't the principles that lead to relationship; it's the relationship that breathes life into the principles.

Knowing His disciples would struggle with this dynamic, Jesus sent His Spirit to establish and maintain this vital personal connection. So this is what you can expect in your life: a deep and abiding experience of God through the presence of the Spirit.

Holy Spirit, keep me connected! I need Your life; I need Your deep and abiding presence every minute of every day. Flow in me now.

day 148

God can do anything, you know—far more than
you could ever imagine or guess or request
in your wildest dreams!
Ephesians 3:20 MSG

Beyond Imagination

People's minds are programmed by fear for small thinking.

And a lot of people carry their small thinking right into their Christian life, never really reaching beyond what they can naturally expect to happen, never getting out on the edge where they need a miracle. Well, the first miracle you need is for God to expand your thinking and your expectation of Him! The Christian life is about far, far more than just being moral, serving faithfully in the church, and going to heaven when you die.

Listen to what God says! Think big. Dream wild. Push your imagination to the brink as you consider how God might use your life to change the world. Got it in your head? Good, now double it. No, multiply it times a hundred. In fact, you can't even comprehend how significant your life is meant to be.

Okay, God, I'm willing to enlarge the smallness of my idea of who You want to be in my life and what You want to do through me.

day 149

No one's ever seen or heard anything like this, never so much as imagined anything quite like it—what God has arranged for those who love him.
1 Corinthians 2:9 MSG

Inconceivable

In the movie *The Princess Bride*, the villain continuously repeats the word *inconceivable*, basically because his thinking is so small that it cannot wrap itself around new possibilities that he has never before experienced.

What you have experienced so far in your life has probably not fully prepared you for the amazing things God has in store for you. In fact, here's another way to divide up the people in the world: those who let their past define their future and those who are able to conceive a future much bigger and broader than their past.

But here's the catch: Hope requires risk. To elevate the scope of your expectation in life demands a willingness to face the risks involved! What risks? First, the risk of being disappointed. (Many people never get past this one.) Second, the risk of what a large future will require of you.

God, I'm willing to take on these risks. And where I'm not, I'm willing to be willing. I don't want to settle for less!

day
150

Faith is the reality of what is hoped for,
the proof of what is not seen.
Hebrews 11:1 HCSB

Take It to the Bank

A life of risk is a life of faith, a life of trusting your future to things that are unseen and intangible. But real. Very, very real!

The willingness to accept this quality of risk into your life acknowledges several realities: First, that life is risky anyway. There is no way to fully protect yourself. The only real question is whether you will take a defensive posture in life or an offensive one. Second, there is something worth hoping for—a vision for something immensely good to happen on planet Earth on your watch.

Finally, risk acknowledges a power much greater than you. The acceptance of risk is the humble response to the bigness of God. He is the safety net—not what you think He will or won't do, but He is Himself the safety net, His person, His character, and His overwhelmingly passionate love for you.

God, grant me certainty in Your promises, trust in Your character, and faith to face risks for Your Kingdom.

Jonathan answered Saul his father and said to him, "Why should he be put to death? What has he done?" Then Saul hurled his spear at him to strike him down; so Jonathan knew that his father had decided to put David to death.
1 Samuel 20:32–33 NASB

day
151

Life on the Line

Jonathan, the crown prince to his father, King Saul, was not afraid of risk. Especially when his integrity and his friendship with David called for it.

No one goes out looking for risk. That is foolishness. But courage is the willingness to do the right thing, even when the consequences are threatening and severe. Jonathan agreed with David to test the state of Saul's heart toward David and see what was there. What he found was a murderous rage lying just barely beneath the regal surface of his father's heart. Jonathan's willingness to champion the innocence of his friend brought him into harm's way.

And the same will be true for you, sooner or later. Integrity will require you to face the risk of harm in order to do what is right.

Help me, God, to pass that test when it comes—to not live in fear but to trust Your ability to protect me in doing the right thing.

day 152

Peter called to him, "Lord, if it's really you,
tell me to come to you by walking on water."
"All right, come," Jesus said.
Matthew 14:28–29 NLT

Life on the Water

Sometimes the risk that is asked of you is the willingness to undertake some initiative for the Kingdom, some act of courage that will advance the cause of Christ on the earth. Sometimes the act is not even "asked" directly from someone else; instead, you simply feel the tug of the Spirit upon your own heart. And you know. You know it's time to act.

Something about the quality of courage elicits God's power in response to your faith. Peter didn't have to step out on a stormy sea. But when he did, God's supernatural power met him there—right in the place of risk—and catapulted him into a level of Kingdom operation he had never before experienced. Probably never before imagined! And so it will be for you when you hear the invitation of God and step out.

God, if it's really You, speak to me and show me how to get out on the water of risk with You. I trust Your intentions toward me.

day
153

By faith Rahab the prostitute received the spies in peace and didn't perish with those who disobeyed.
Hebrews 11:31 HCSB

Irrational Faith

Faith sees beyond the natural realm and the rational mind. Do you remember this woman Rahab? She was a prostitute—not exactly your first pick for a mighty woman of faith. But appearances can be deceiving!

Rahab received enemy spies from Israel into her home. There was no reasonable expectation that Israel stood any chance whatsoever in conquering her city. And why would Rahab even want them to succeed against her own people? It doesn't add up.

It was an irrational faith that somehow caused this woman to see that (1) God was on the side of her enemies, (2) that Israel would accomplish an impossible victory, and (3) that she would have a future among those enemies. The result? Rahab became part of the lineage of Jesus! That's the power of risky faith.

God, please give me the kind of vision that exceeds my rational, self-protective instincts and catapults me into destiny.

day 154

When she could hide him no longer, she got a papyrus basket for him and coated it with tar and pitch. Then she placed the child in it and put it among the reeds along the bank of the Nile.
Exodus 2:3 NIV

Jochebed's Gamble

You may not recognize the name of Jochebed, but you probably recognize the result of the risks she faced. His name was Moses, her son, and he was bound to die at the hands of Pharaoh's minions before his first birthday. Whether it was purely the protective instinct of a mother or Jochebed's realization that there was great destiny riding upon her son is not clear. What is clear is that she defied this unjust law and risked her life for what she knew was right.

Then she took another risky gamble, placing her newborn son in a floating basket on the Nile River, with the uncertain hope that the Egyptian princess would have mercy upon him. Her faith was rewarded, and it changed the very course of history for a nation! You never know the full effects of one act of risky righteousness.

God, if You will help me be faithful in the little risks I encounter, I know You will bring big results that affect others for good.

day 155

When Jesus heard that John had been put in prison, he returned to Galilee . . . From that time on Jesus began to preach, "Repent, for the kingdom of heaven is near."
Matthew 4:12, 17 NIV

Extraterrestrial Invasion

Earth truly is the subject of an extraterrestrial invasion! But it isn't Martians or other sci-fi critters. God Himself is reclaiming His own rightful possession.

In the beginning, earth was a true expression of the Kingdom of heaven—a physical representation of the spiritual realities that make up God's realm. That expression was lost. "Bent," as C. S. Lewis would say. And for thousands of years, God was reaching to restore a people who would begin to reclaim its lost heritage.

But it took the coming of Jesus to really bring a substantial shift in the equation. His purpose was fully bound up in the restoration of heaven's rule on earth. His message was, "Change your old thinking, your old identity. Remember who you really are—sons and daughters of heaven! My Kingdom is available to you."

God, restore us! Restore me! Let my life be a heavenly impetus that rekindles people's hunger for their true home.

day 156

The seed that fell on the hard path represents those who hear the Good News about the Kingdom and don't understand it . . . The good soil represents the hearts of those who truly accept God's message.
Matthew 13:19, 23 NLT

Hard Rock Alley

Jesus chose simple little stories (parables) to give profound insights into the culture of heaven and its implications for men and women. Matthew 13 records a whole string of stories that open up a window of illumination into God's realm.

In this story, the seed represents God's message of restoration, the packets of life-giving truth that will transform the brokenness of people's lives. Several types of "soil" within people's hearts resist God's message and remain broken. A hard-hearted condition shies away from the foreignness of heaven's culture and remains unchanged.

But there are others who "have ears to hear" and receive Jesus' message with gladness. Where is your life being radically redeemed by the power of heaven's ways? Where do you resist that kind of change? Does your life confirm the "nearness" of heaven?

Have full and unfettered access to my life, God. Let my heart respond warmly to every seed of truth and love You offer today.

The kingdom of heaven is like a man who sowed good seed in his field. But while everyone was sleeping, his enemy came and sowed weeds among the wheat, and went away.
Matthew 13:24–25 NIV

day
157

Put on Your 3-D Glasses

In this scenario, God describes the two Kingdom realities at work in the world—the outgrowth of heaven and the outgrowth of hell. The conflict between these two realms is real and violent and hidden.

You know how a pair of 3-D glasses enables you to see an image that's hidden in a blur of color? That's God's desire for you—to be able to clearly and easily perceive which is which. Which words and actions and motivations are consistent with heaven and which are opposed to it? Without the glasses, it's very confusing!

The story goes on to describe how the owner allows both the wheat and the weeds to grow until the harvest. In the same way, both heaven and hell remain active in this world until Jesus returns, but the man or woman with Kingdom eyes will discern the difference.

God, give me Kingdom eyes to discern these two realms at work and to align myself fully with Your purposes today.

day 158

The kingdom of heaven is like a mustard seed that a man took and sowed in his field . . . The kingdom of heaven is like yeast that a woman took and mixed into 50 pounds of flour until it spread through all of it.
Matthew 13:31, 33 HCSB

A Little Goes a Long Way

This is one of the mysteries of the Kingdom: Things are not always what they seem. What appears wise and monumental in this world is often silly and inconsequential in the Kingdom realm. Conversely, the most potent and dynamic forces of God's Kingdom often appear weak and ridiculous in this world. But of course they aren't!

At the time the Bible was written, the mustard seed was the smallest seed that a farmer would typically work with. The irony was that this tiny seed produced a much larger plant than most seeds many times its size—a tree that reached as tall as ten feet! Similarly, a pinch of yeast works its way through many loaves of bread.

In this way, the Kingdom of God makes tremendous advances through disproportionately small acts of obedience and faith.

God, take my little acts of faith and obedience and multiply their effect in the unseen realm. Let me be a world-changer.

God's kingdom is like a treasure hidden in a field for years and then accidentally found by a trespasser . . . Or, God's kingdom is like a jewel merchant on the hunt for excellent pearls.
Matthew 13:44–45 MSG

day 159

Treasure Island

Heaven is an absolute treasure—an island filled with chest after chest of wealth beyond imagination. It awakens the senses, it captures the affections, it makes you fully alive! Once you get a glimpse of the treasure, it ceases instantly to be a fairy tale; from that moment onward, everything else pales in significance. Your heart is owned by a treasure grander than any pirate's loot.

Some stumble onto Kingdom treasure almost by accident. They didn't even know they were looking for God's realm, and yet God found them and invited them in. Others, God awakens their hunger from deep inside their spirit so that they search and search until they find it! Whichever it is, Jesus says, the result is the same: They sell everything else to possess that one priceless item. Have you sold out yet?

God, You have my heart—You and You alone! There's just nothing else that compares with the true wealth You bring to my life.

day 160

The kingdom of heaven is like a dragnet cast into the sea, and gathering fish of every kind; and when it was filled, they drew it up on the beach; and they sat down and gathered the good fish into containers, but the bad they threw away.
Matthew13:47–48 NASB

Fishing Break

Jesus offers some commentary that is a bit intimidating at first glance: "Not everyone who says to me, 'Lord, Lord,' will enter the kingdom of heaven, but only he who does the will of my Father who is in heaven" (Matthew 7:21 NIV). The truth is that no one knows the absolute heart of another except God. And what's vital to realize is that you don't have to; it really is God's job, and He does it very well.

What *is* your job? As a Kingdom man or woman, you get the privilege of inviting in all comers, of casting wide the "net" of God's affection and letting all come who want to experience Him. You don't have to figure out who is "in" and who is "out." Too many people get caught up in that stuff.

God, it is the deep prayer of my heart that
You would draw many, many people to
Yourself. Make me a "fisher" of people.

The kingdom of God does not come with your careful observation, nor will people say, "Here it is," or "There it is," because the Kingdom of God is within you.
Luke 17:20–21 NIV

day 161

Secret but Powerful

When Jesus was on earth and as people began to recognize Him as the Messiah, the Savior, many began to pressure Him about becoming an earthly king and establishing a political kingdom there in Israel. But that was not at all Jesus' plan.

He knew that His Kingdom was a spiritual reality and was meant to change people from the inside out (not the outside in). Because it works in an unseen dimension, many people miss it. But the power of it is that it cannot be stopped: It lives inside you.

Political powers come and go, but the restoring life of heaven can flow in any nation, under any government, even hostile ones. This is the brilliance of God and the beauty of His plan. You need to know that the Kingdom invasion taking place now on planet Earth is vested inside you!

God, thank You for planting Your eternal Kingdom life in me. Let it grow and influence and draw many to You in quiet, powerful ways.

day 162

The Kingdom of heaven will be like 10 virgins who took their lamps and went out to meet the groom . . . Therefore be alert, because you don't know either the day or the hour.
Matthew 25:1, 13 HCSB

Pay Attention

There is a character quality that is quite essential for Kingdom effectiveness, but you won't find it in many lists of personality styles or virtues. It's the quality of paying attention. Paying attention to spiritual realities as much as natural ones. Paying attention not just to events but to relationships, not just to circumstances but to the meaning of those circumstances.

Jesus called it being alert. And it takes determination to remain alert in the midst of the busyness and chaos that make up much of what we call life. Those who are determined to remain alert position themselves to partner with God—to know what He's doing and cooperate with Him. Like the virgins who watched diligently for the groom, your attention to Kingdom movement will release His purposes in your life.

Wake up my spirit, God, so I can pay attention to You and remain alert. I don't want to be oblivious to what You're doing.

day
163

You're blessed when your commitment to God provokes persecution. The persecution drives you even deeper into God's kingdom.
Matthew 5:10 MSG

Jesus Freak

Determination is particularly called for when you're experiencing pain. In fact, no one can take the heat without it. Your commitment to God and His purposes will bring you into situations where your values are in total conflict with the values of others. Your passion for God or for His ways may not be appreciated and may bring reprisals. This can happen on campus or in your office or pretty much anywhere.

The power of persecution is that it will expose what's in your heart. If your convictions are conditional, you'll find yourself alienated from God's Kingdom. But if your convictions are rooted in your very being and identity, then you'll find yourself driven into a deeper place of intimacy with God and solidarity with His Kingdom purposes. This is the way God brings something good out of something bad.

God, You know I'm not looking for persecution or pain,
but I'm willing to persevere through that to find
new intimacy with You.

day 164

Let your heart therefore be loyal to the LORD our God, to walk in His statutes and keep His commandments, as at this day.
1 Kings 8:61 NKJV

Go the Distance

It's one thing to start strong. It's quite another to finish strong!

In the history of God's people, there are periods of loyal faithfulness and then longer periods where people forgot God and His ways and lost their passion, at great cost to themselves and their community. This verse is part of King Solomon's charge to the people of Israel as he dedicated the grand, massive Temple he had just built for the worship of God.

Some of those who heard Solomon's voice actually did go the distance and live a life of determined loyalty to God. Others did not. In fact, Solomon himself did not finish well.

Finishing well is about more than even your own prosperity. The verse before this one highlights that it's the honor of God that is at stake among those who bear His name.

God, keep my heart strong and my head clear to keep You at the center of my affections—for Your honor and my blessing.

day
165

To the faithful you show yourself faithful, to the blameless you show yourself blameless.
Psalm 18:25 NIV

What Goes Around . . .

You've heard the expression "What goes around comes around." In other words, the way you act has great effect upon the way others act toward you. Justice has a way of catching up with people, usually in this lifetime but for certain in the next. And it even applies to your relationship with God.

God is, of course, always faithful and completely blameless. However, not everyone gets to experience that side of God. Some folks resist God and resist God and resist God, and find that God cannot be manipulated. This passage goes on to say, "but to the crooked you show yourself shrewd" (v. 26 NIV). Which is to say that you can't put anything over on God; He's just a bit smarter than you. Your faithfulness will, however, be rewarded by the incomparable experience of God's unending faithfulness toward you!

God, I want to know Your faithfulness in my life; help me to remain determined in my pursuit of You all my days.

day 166

Do not fear what you are about to suffer. Behold, the devil is about to cast some of you into prison, so that you will be tested, and you will have tribulation for ten days. Be faithful until death, and I will give you the crown of life.
Revelation 2:10 NASB

Fearless Faith

Determination is based upon your vision of the prize at the end of the race. No one wants to suffer or face a violent death—only a supernatural courage can empower such determination. Courage . . . and an unwavering vision of the "crown of life" that awaits you—the life of God Himself.

Your potential sufferings may not be prison and death. The persecution God carries you through might be slanderous criticism or the betrayal of a friend or being passed over for a promotion. God allows some of these circumstances to test your heart and increase your determination to do what's right, to stand by your convictions. Daniel 11:32 says that "the people who know their God shall be strong, and carry out great exploits" (NKJV). You will be one of these people!

Yes, God, with Your help I wil be one of these people. I will know You and accomplish great things through You.

day 167

A faithful man will be richly blessed, but one eager to get rich will not go unpunished.
Proverbs 28:20 NIV

No Shortcuts

There really aren't very many shortcuts in life. If any. But since people usually want more than they have—and don't want to wait to get it—they look for shortcuts all the time. Consider the staggering amount of personal debt that people accumulate. Or consider the reams of books that promise shortcuts to get rich, to lose weight, to learn a new language, to win friends and influence people. The list goes on and on.

Don't be suckered into false promises. There is no substitute for faithfulness. Setting your heart upon a worthy goal and then sticking determinedly to it will inevitably bring blessings. This certainly holds true in the spiritual life and the New Rebellion. There are no shortcuts to faithfulness. Those who attempt them are "punished" by disappointment and failure.

I am determined to life a life of steady faithfulness, to put in the work and the prayer to build relationships and change my world.

day 168

Who then is a faithful and sensible slave, whom his master has put in charge of his household, to give them food at the proper time? That slave whose master finds him working when he comes will be rewarded.
Matthew 24:45–46 HCSB

It Makes Sense

Let's be honest. Sometimes you get tired of doing the things you know are right. Tired of serving others, tired of reading your Bible, tired of reaching for your destiny. What you do when you are weary and disappointed with life is the defining mark of a man or woman of determination.

It doesn't make sense to put out a lot of effort for a period of time and then quit. It does make sense to stay the course of truth and blessing even when you're tired. Even when God isn't doing the things that you expect or want. But it's not easy.

That's why life is a partnership. It doesn't hinge on your great strength but on His! Faithfulness is where your will to follow God intersects with His empowering grace to sustain you, equip you, encourage you, and love you.

God, I need Your strength today to stay the course and be a faithful servant. You are my constant source and truest friend.

If you walk before me in integrity of heart and uprightness, as David your father did, and do all I command and observe my decrees and laws, I will establish your royal throne over Israel forever.
1 Kings 9:4–5 NIV

day 169

Can God Trust You?

People who have walked with God for any amount of time know their hearts are fickle. "Prone to wander, Lord, I feel it. Prone to leave the God I love," a famous hymn phrases it. Yet God is in the business of restoring lives with damaged rudders! He is, in fact, intent on making you a man or woman of lasting integrity.

The New Rebellion will be built by those who consistently live in a Godward posture. They aren't perfect and stumble often, but they stumble *toward* God, not away from Him. Over time, they find such delight in His ways that their character runs in patterns deep and wide over the contours of their souls. Partner with God this day in the hidden places of your heart so that what others see can only be called integrity.

God, shape me and mold my heart so that every attitude, word, and action accurately portrays Your passion in my world.

day 170

I know, my God, that you examine our hearts and rejoice when you find integrity there.
1 Chronicles 29:17 NLT

X-Ray Vision

It is simultaneously terrifying and securing to know that God has unfettered access to your heart, that His gaze penetrates like an X-ray. Terrifying, because you're often ashamed of what He'll find. And securing, because although He knows the worst, He remains committed to you with a passion that defies reason!

Ultimately, God's examinations empower your life as a world-changer. His delight in integrity releases a surge of desire within you to live out that integrity. And His confidence that the Spirit of God can actually establish integrity within you is a securing force that positions your heart to succeed. So embrace His searching, revel in His empowering grace. Send your worship back to the One who builds your character by the infusions of His.

God, here I am. I'll never run in fear from Your gaze!
You know me completely, and still Your love for me
won't quit. I want to be like You.

day 171

The LORD said to Satan, "Have you considered My servant Job? For there is no one like him on the earth, a blameless and upright man fearing God and turning away from evil. And he still holds fast his integrity, although you incited Me against him to ruin him without cause."
Job 2:3 NASB

Take the Heat—See What's There

If you could trade lives with anyone in the Bible, the sign-up for Job's life would be pretty short!

But everyone gets his turn at times of pain and suffering. Some suffering is extraordinary, and some is pretty ordinary. But the point is that God chooses. And the women and men after God's heart learn to take the heat; they learn to let the pressure release the fragrance of Christ from their lives.

Stress and pain have a way of showing you what's inside. Rebels of courage don't shrink back from the examination! And neither should you. What doesn't kill you, makes you stronger. Job discovered this to be true, and even though he was shaken to the core of his being, his integrity held true. How about you?

God, secure my heart with courage so that I won't cut bait and run when You test my soul. When I'm squeezed, let it be You who comes out!

day 172

He who walks with integrity walks securely, but he who perverts his ways will become known.
Proverbs 10:9 NKJV

It's All Going to Come Out

You're reading this devotional because you want to live on purpose. You want to make a difference in the world by loving and serving God with everything you have! Right?

Good. Because that's God's heart too. But if there's one thing that will trip you up and disqualify you from building the Kingdom, it's hiding. Even though you know you can't hide from God, there is still a powerful urge to separate your public image from your private image. You have to understand this current and its pull on your soul in order to resist it.

Integrity is when there is no gap between the private image (the real "you" when you're alone) and the public image (the "you" everyone else sees). This consistency of life takes away fear and sets your heart free to enjoy living.

Close the gap, dear God, between who I am
and who I want to be. Only You can
anchor my life in authenticity.

day
173

A God-loyal life keeps you on track;
sin dumps the wicked in the ditch.
Proverbs 13:6 MSG

Guardrails Are Nice on a Mountain

It's pretty simple, really. Righteousness protects your life; sin trashes it. In light of that, why would anybody willingly let themselves be thrown brutally into a ditch? Why does it happen?

Sin is nothing less than thinking you know better than God. Everyone makes choices based on what they believe will bring good things to them. Those who trust God do the things that, even when they run against their instincts, actually work. They protect you; they bring blessing; they keep you on track. Conversely, sin deceives, promising what it can never deliver.

So get a clue! This day, live wide open for God. Through integrity, make God-loyal decisions. This kind of obedience will be the guardrails on today's mountains, protecting you from many hazards.

God, You're the One who's designed this life;
I'm going to bet my life that You know how it
works best. Keep me true and loyal to You.

day 174

Set an example of good works yourself, with integrity and dignity in your teaching. Your message is to be sound beyond reproach, so that the opponent will be ashamed, having nothing bad to say about us.
Titus 2:7–8 HCSB

No Dirt to Dig

You know how the political arena works, right? It's not so much about establishing your own character as it is about tearing down the character of your opponent. Finding dirt on the other guy is big business! Public servants are assumed to lack integrity, and all too often it's true.

God builds His Kingdom upon men and women who have died to their own selfish interests, people like you. You aren't pursuing your own gratification anymore and doing the things that bring shame and embarrassment. Instead, you are filled with God's Spirit, living out His purposes on the earth. Both your message and your lifestyle are consistent with the character of heaven, so that you won't bring reproach upon the name of Jesus!

God, keep refining my heart from the things that would hinder me or discredit You. Let my life shine with Your purity today.

day 175

A wife of noble character who can find? She is worth far more than rubies. Her husband has full confidence in her and lacks nothing of value.
Proverbs 31:10–11 NIV

Gateway to Confidence

Perhaps the most valuable reward of integrity is trust. The more God shapes your life and brings you into alignment with His own character, the more other people respect you and are willing to place their confidence in you. The trust of others is a priceless gift.

On the other hand, if you find others reluctant to entrust you with responsibility, then it may be an indicator that your integrity is not yet fully established. Like most things in the Christian life, integrity is not a product of mere human effort. Nor is it solely a gift from God. Instead, it is a heavenly partnership that combines God's ability with your availability and then colors your character, over time, with the hue of heaven. Your reward is the confidence of others.

God, I'm ready to be shaped and molded by You.
My will belongs to You. I set my heart to obey You
and follow Your ways.

day 176

We know that the whole creation has been groaning together with labor pains until now. And not only that, but we ourselves who have the Spirit as the firstfruits—we also groan within ourselves, eagerly waiting for adoption, the redemption of our bodies.
Romans 8:22–23 HCSB

The Now and the Not Yet

As much as the New Rebellion is about God's movement across the earth, there is still a very real and important sense in which God's people are living out their days within the tension of waiting. This is the backdrop against which God calls us to action.

When you first accepted Jesus' invitation into the life of the Kingdom, you participated—in that instant—in the redemptive power of God, transforming your spirit from death to life. But the fullness of your spiritual redemption will be seen only when you cross the chasm of death and see Him face-to-face in eternity.

In the meantime, we feel the tension between who we are meant to be and who we yet remain. And we wait, with the hope and expectation that the Kingdom of God moves forward, slowly, but with increasing momentum.

God, when my heart groans within me, longing for the fullness of my redemption, I will trust You and embrace the purpose of today.

day 177

Since ancient times no one has heard, no ear has perceived, no eye has seen any God besides you, who acts on behalf of those who wait for him.
Isaiah 64:4 NIV

A Severe Mercy

Within the cosmic waiting that God's people experience on planet Earth, there is a very personal waiting that anchors human dependency upon God. And as such, waiting is a skill to be learned. Over time, you learn not to rush zealously, blindly ahead in pursuit of the Kingdom. Rather, you look and listen for what God's up to, and then you join Him in what He's doing!

The mercy and kindness of God are poised to move within our world, coiled up with expectant purpose until being unleashed with goodness upon men and women everywhere. The extent of God's lavish intentions toward His people are only hinted at. But in order to be the vehicle through which He demonstrates His kindness, you must, yes, wait upon Him.

Wait for what? Wait for His timing, wait for His ways and wisdom, wait for His presence.

God, I don't wait very well! But as I submit my will to Your highest purpose, I expect You to release me into divine action.

day 178

I've kept my feet on the ground, I've cultivated a quiet heart. Like a baby content in its mother's arms, my soul is a baby content.
Psalm 131:2 MSG

Learning to Wait Well

The cultural currents that wrap around you and tug at your soul hate waiting. Busyness is the order of the day! Frantic rushing here and there, the futile effort to get just one more task squeezed into your day.

But this is why you're a Rebel! Say "no" to the noise and clamor of those voices and carve out quietness of heart, the core from which divine purpose flows. This spiritual secret has always empowered men and women of God to go the distance—learning to still the soul like a sleeping baby and wait well.

This contented, Godward orientation allows you to hear the beat of His heart, just like a resting child. Then, with His passion and direction, you will affect your world, moving to the beat of a different heart!

God, draw me close and quiet my soul, quiet enough to hear what's on Your heart this day. Then send me out in quiet purpose.

Regarding the ambassadors of the princes of Babylon, whom they sent to him to inquire about the wonder that was done in the land, God withdrew from him, in order to test him, that He might know all that was in his heart.
2 Chronicles 32:31 NKJV

day
179

Disclosure

Hezekiah was king of Judah—a godly leader who followed after God, in marked contrast to his father, Ahaz. Toward the end of his life, he prepared to welcome Babylonian envoys who had come to inquire about God's miraculous works. Right at this crucial juncture, the Bible says that God withdrew from Hezekiah. Why in the world would God do that?

Fortunately, the Bible answers that question. He did it to test him and know what was in the king's heart. Did God not know? Of course He did. The unveiling of Hezekiah's heart was for Hezekiah's benefit! So that he could understand his own heart! And this is the gift of waiting seasons in your life as well. When God's presence lifts, it's time to search your heart and then search for His.

God, I don't always understand my own heart, but You do! Help me to remain fully dependent upon You and empowered by You.

day 180

Until the time that his word came to pass,
the word of the LORD tested him.
Psalm 105:19 NKJV

It's Pass/Fail, but There's a Makeup

This time the testing came to a man named Joseph, and the experience was such a pivotal one that King David wrote about it almost a thousand years later. What David saw in Joseph's experience (as well as his own) was that the promises of God hang over you, often for many years, testing your faith and urging you onward. This kind of test was not a comfortable one, but it was essential to developing the kind of courage and tenacity required in their lives and yours.

You don't always pass God's tests, but God never gives up on you. There's always a makeup test just around the corner until you learn the important lesson. God's lessons qualify you for your destiny. You, too, have promises hanging over your life; they will test you, but they will eventually come to pass.

God, help me pass the tests that You bring into this day. Let me never give up on Your promises over my life.

day 181

Hope deferred makes the heart sick.
Proverbs 13:12 NASB

Heartsickness—Real but Not Fatal

When you're waiting for God to fulfill His promises to you, you often face discouragement. When weeks turn into months, and months turn into years, it can seem like God's ignoring you or maybe even forgotten you! But He isn't, and He hasn't. Hope is the most powerful weapon you have, and it's backed up by the character of heaven, even when hope is delayed and heartsickness grows.

This is when it's most important to not lose your grip on hope. Yes, heartsickness is real, but hope will not fail you. You *will* be released into your calling; you *will* be a world-changer. And the challenge of today might just be to change your own inner world by not giving up. The ability to conquer your own inner battles will qualify you to engage larger spiritual battles in the days to come.

God, I thank You that You're more powerful than any sickness of heart, and that hope will heal and strengthen and empower my life.

day 182

When dreams come true, there is life and joy.
Proverbs 13:12 NLT

God Makes Good on Promises

Fortunately, yesterday's proverb doesn't end with sick hearts; instead, there is a vibrant encouragement that God's dreams do come true! And the dreams God has planted inside you will satisfy your soul like nothing else. But it all hinges upon hope.

Hope is the ability to believe God when all your circumstances say otherwise, when it appears there is no possible way for God's promises to come true. Hope is the grace to wait well. So no matter what you're waiting for, trust God and keep reaching for the right dreams. Don't allow discouragement any place in your heart, but keep pressing through difficulty until God's purposes come to light. And they will.

God knows what you are made for. Your job is to find what you're made for and to follow Him through wonderful times and horrendous times, until His Kingdom comes.

Thank You for the dreams You have over my life, God.
My eyes are on You, to hope and believe and become
the Kingdom Rebel You intend.

The one thing I ask of the LORD—the thing I seek most—is to live in the house of the LORD all the days of my life, delighting in the LORD's perfections and meditating in his Temple.
Psalm 27:4 NLT

day 183

One Thing

As one advertisement says, "Life comes at you fast." So many things compete for your attention, your affections, your time. Sometimes it feels as if you've lost your sense of direction. Rather than your living life, life is living you! But above all things, there is one priority—an obsession of the soul—that stands tall, and it is the Lord Himself! He is the one thing that makes sense in this world.

So perhaps it's time to sort through the many components of your days and realign your priorities. While the world obsesses over time management, God's people are called to priority management. If there is one thing that belongs at the center of life, the one thing that rightfully calls for your most earnest pursuit, it is God's presence. Seek His nearness! Delight in His beauty.

There is none like You, God. You have the chief place in my passions; You are the prize that I seek today in everything I do.

day 184

Jesus answered and said to her, "Martha, Martha, you are worried and troubled about many things. But one thing is needed, and Mary has chosen that good part, which will not be taken away from her."
Luke 10:41–42 NKJV

One Thing Too

King David found his "one thing." And so did another young woman named Mary.

It's a common story—the distractions of Martha, trying to do all the right things but somehow missing the most important thing of all. But it's a very uncommon reality to find men and women today who authentically live out a Mary-motivation, who make significant room in their lives to sit at His feet and just be there. To be all there.

In contrast, many God-followers practice fast-food spirituality, trying to gulp down a full "meal" of God's presence in between the many other demands of the day. But this book is for Rebels with a cause. The cause is Christ, and the Rebellion is against the currents of busyness that want to define your life. Be different. Find your one thing and don't let go.

God, I'm taking my place beside Mary today!
Even if no one else does, I will make
You the one thing I pursue most.

Brethren, I do not regard myself as having laid hold of it yet; but one thing I do: forgetting what lies behind and reaching forward to what lies ahead, I press on toward the goal for the prize of the upward call of God in Christ Jesus.
Philippians 3:13–14 NASB

day 185

One Thing Again

First David, then Mary, now Paul. Do you see a pattern here? Paul had about as many responsibilities as you can imagine—dozens of churches needing his oversight, new cities yet to hear the good news, life-threatening opposition all around. But in the midst of these cares and concerns, Paul's heart was gripped by one consuming passion: the person and presence of Jesus Christ.

That all-compelling prize motivated Paul to lay aside all the fears, all the uncertainties, and fix his attention on God. Obedience to this call was his one thing. What's yours? To hold on to Christ as Paul did, you also will have to dispense with lesser things. You, too, will need to forget what lies behind and reach for the goal. Salvation isn't the end; salvation is the beginning!

God, help me now to see anything in my life that obscures or distracts me from the priority of You. You are my first love.

day 186

How do you benefit if you gain the whole world but lose your own soul in the process? Is anything worth more than your soul?
Matthew 16:26 NLT

The Alternative to One Thing

Many people spend a lifetime pursuing things that may be good but not good enough. Not nearly as good as the One Thing. The pursuit of status or wealth or personal power may reward you in materialistic ways. But they will cost you in the realm that really matters—the life of the soul. And, as Jesus asks pointedly, "Is anything worth more than your soul?"

The most important things in life are usually the least urgent. They can easily be put off, particularly when you feel people's expectations of you to run after the same trivial things everyone else pursues. But when you consider the treasure of knowing Christ and finding yourself in Him, what does the rest really matter? Your soul was fashioned for one overarching purpose—intimacy with God. It's time to live on purpose.

Lead me, God. Show me the secret ways of Your Kingdom.
Help me to see what's most valuable and give
myself to what's precious.

Jesus . . . said, "There's one thing left: Go sell whatever you own and give it to the poor. All your wealth will then be heavenly wealth. And come follow me." The man's face clouded over.

Mark 10:21–22 MSG

day 187

Competition for the One Thing

The young man Jesus was talking with was no Pharisee. He was not working the religious system for his own power. He was sincere; he earnestly wanted to live a life pleasing to God. And Jesus' love and compassion were kindled toward him. Yet He also knew that this man's spiritual journey was obstructed by a competing loyalty, a higher love than his love for God. And with all the tenderness of a physician, Jesus put His finger right on that place of misshapen priority, his money.

The man was very rich. And his commitment to his money exceeded his commitment to the Kingdom of God. What about with you? Are there possessions or dreams or activities that grip your heart more than the treasure of heaven? If so, Jesus speaks to you as well, "Let it go. Come follow Me."

Cleanse me. Rinse me. Strip away all the vain pursuits that clutter my soul. Let me run wholeheartedly after You, God!

day 188

I hold this against you: You have forsaken your first love.
Revelation 2:4 NIV

One Love

Jesus spoke this bold confrontation to the Ephesian church. Most of this letter was actually a commendation—these were women and men who had served God faithfully, who embraced the truth, and who resisted distraction and corruption. But somehow they had come to the place where they were serving God out of duty instead of delight. Most followers of Jesus know this feeling at certain times.

But God will never be content with righteous behavior alone. It's the heart that He's jealous for; He yearns for the freshness and joyful wonder of a "first-love" relationship. The excitement of new love arises out of the joy of discovery . . . and with God, there are always reams more to discover. Stagnancy with God comes only with apathy, but love is untiring in its pursuit. And in its joy.

Open my eyes, God, to see amazing new vistas of Your beauty this day, to glimpse new realities of Your character and Your wonderful ways.

day 189

Love the Lord your God with all your heart, with all your soul, and with all your mind. This is the greatest and most important commandment.
Matthew 22:37–38 HCSB

A Consuming Passion

Well, if God's priorities weren't clear before, they are now. Jesus took everything that God had revealed about Himself to date—the Abrahamic covenant, the Law of Moses, the revelation of the prophets, and everything else—and summed the core of God's heart up in one sentence. Love God. Love Him completely. Love Him obsessively. Let every facet of your being, every aspect that makes up who you are, belong 100 percent to Him.

So what does that look like? How will that consuming passion be expressed through your experiences, your relationships, and your choices today? It's a probing question, and frankly, it is *the* question of your life. It all belongs to Him—your work, your exercise, your friendships, your downtime—it all exists for the purpose of communicating your undying love for God.

All right, God, You see my heart. You know my hunger to love in practical, meaningful ways. Show me how to live my love for You today.

day 190

It is God's privilege to conceal things and the king's privilege to discover them.
Proverbs 25:2 NLT

Hide-and-Seek

Have you noticed that God's ways are often mystifying? Why does He allow bad things to happen; why doesn't He bring more of the good things you desire? Does it sometimes feel like God is playing hide-and-seek with you?

Well, He is. God wants to be pursued. Not because He's insecure, but because He is the sum of all love, and He desires to be loved in return. So God invites you into the quest of a lifetime: the pursuit of heavenly intimacy.

God longs to share His mysteries with you. It's true! The question is this: Are you motivated to search long and wide enough to discover them? When you do, you'll be drawn into that much more fellowship with the Eternal. He really does offer you His heart in friendship.

God, can it be true? Would You begin to share Your perspective with me and open my eyes to the beauty of Your mysteries? I can't wait.

day 191

"Yes, when you get serious about finding me and want it more than anything else, I'll make sure you won't be disappointed." GOD'S Decree.
Jeremiah 29:13–14 MSG

You Won't Be Disappointed

Your most authentic longings were crafted by God Himself—they aren't there by mere chance. And because He placed your passions within you, He faces no uncertainty trying to figure out how to satisfy you! God is determined to be the greatest satisfaction, the greatest pleasure you could ever experience. He will not disappoint you.

But your heart can't be fed by God if you ignore Him. He will not force His blessings upon you; they must be searched for by people who are intent upon Him. Those who are casual in their pursuit—recreational Christians, you might call them—aren't bound to discover much. But God assures you that those who are serious about finding Him will be nourished deeply and abundantly! He puts His reputation on the line for you.

God, teach me how to search for You and how to find You. I want to know You so completely! Open the eyes of my heart.

day 192

Acknowledge the God of your father, and serve him with wholehearted devotion and with a willing mind, for the LORD searches every heart and understands every motive behind the thoughts. If you seek him, he will be found by you.
1 Chronicles 28:9 NIV

Wholehearted

The thing is, you can't play God. You can't schmooze Him, flatter Him, network Him, or pull the wool over His eyes. He sees the heart; nothing is hidden from His gaze. He's not looking for perfection, but He longs intensely to find a pure desire in your heart for Him. He wants your motivation to be a wholehearted devotion, just as with King Solomon.

What does it mean to seek Him wholeheartedly? It doesn't mean that you never have doubts or discouragements, but it does mean that you know where your heart's home is. You know to whom you belong, and you keep coming back to your first love, God Himself. You're not trying to use God to get other things; instead, your greatest longing is God. To know Him and be known by Him. To love Him more consistently and authentically.

God, this day I choose You. My life, I devote to You.
You will always have my whole heart—not just
once a week, but all my days.

I must arise now and go about the city; in the streets and in the squares I must seek him whom my soul loves.
Song of Solomon 3:2 NASB

day 193

Compelled

When you have made the Lord your deepest devotion, then being with Him becomes a deep yearning, an inescapable longing. If a day or two go by without authentic connection, an ache begins to well up in your soul—a heart cry for the object of your passion! There's no escaping it.

Compelled. There is no other way to describe it! The bond of child to Father is defining, and you will never be satisfied outside the tangible expression of His unending affection for you. And yours in return. This is your truest identity, and so you are compelled to seek Him and find Him and cherish Him and worship Him. Never ignore or squelch this yearning—it is your lifeline to life eternal. Turn your passions loose in the pursuit of the divine; this is what you are made for.

God, thank You for drawing my soul after Yours. Thank You for this precious lovesickness that drives my soul to You time after time.

day 194

The young lions lack and suffer hunger; but those who seek the LORD shall not lack any good thing.
Psalm 34:10 NKJV

A Good Reward

God's personalized promise to you, lifelong, is that if He is the object of your quest—not wealth or accomplishment or other pleasures—you will never run short of His goodness.

Now, it is possible to genuinely pursue God yet feel like you're lacking good things. It is possible to suffer hardship and loss, even the loss of life itself! Is this a failure on God's promise? No, and here's why. There is no difficulty or suffering that does not contain a doorway to greater intimacy with God.

In fact, some of the "good things" God most fervently wants to grant you (think about the fruit of the Spirit like patience, faithfulness, and self-control) can be obtained *only* by walking through hardship and coming out the other side. There are no shortcuts to those particular good gifts from God.

Help me to see Your goodness, God, when things are difficult and my life is uncomfortable. Help me to trust and receive Your rewards.

day 195

The heart of the discerning acquires knowledge;
the ears of the wise seek it out.
Proverbs 18:15 NIV

The Only Way to Wisdom

No one becomes wise by accident. Deep wisdom is the result of seriously and intentionally setting your heart to search it out. Discernment is the dedication to acquire truth and to understand how truths fit together. Discernment is recognized by an uncommon insight into things that are hidden. And the point is that those caught up in a life quest to know God and understand His ways will uncover things that are hidden from others who don't search.

Life can be lived reactively—just responding to people and situations as they arise. But that is a meager existence. Instead, women and men determined to become wise take the initiative of proactive pursuit. They seek, they uncover, they grapple, they wrestle. And over time, God rewards the effort with a growing wisdom.

I don't want to be lazy or foolish, God. Give me a heart that loves wisdom and increases wisdom through every experience of life.

day 196

She went ahead and saddled the donkey, ordering her servant, "Take the lead—and go as fast as you can; I'll tell you if you're going too fast." And so off she went. She came to the Holy Man at Mount Carmel. 2 Kings 4:24–25 MSG

In Pursuit

This woman, known in Scripture as the Shunammite, was desperate for God. Her only son, himself a gift from God, had suddenly died, and this woman of faith had a quest. She would not be denied. Without even taking the time to tell her husband what she was doing, she set off for the prophet Elisha at top speed. She would not tell her business to Elisha's servant. And even when Elisha had sent his servant to her house with his staff to touch the boy, she would not leave Elisha. She was determined to find God through God's representative and to obtain the object of her quest. And obtain it she did.

Sometimes, you just can't quit. You can't be distracted or diverted. You can't settle for half a solution. You must have God and nothing less.

God, give me the same desperation and commitment that the Shunammite woman had. Where nothing else will do but You and You alone.

day 197

I don't think there's any comparison between the present hard times and the coming good times.
Romans 8:18 MSG

Bird's-Eye View

When the Navy is training men and women for its intensive SEAL unit, they don't say, "Welcome aboard," and begin to wine and dine you. It's no invitation to vacation! Instead, on day one, they do something like throw you in a helicopter and drop you fifty feet into the ocean for a day and a night. It's called training, and it prepares these folks to accomplish fantastic missions under the toughest of conditions. Not unlike your spiritual life!

Pain is God's tool to prepare you for wonderful things to come. He's no masochist; He doesn't thrive on tormenting His children. Instead, He understands the big picture in ways you don't that pain prepares. And those who successfully navigate painful situations are those God can trust for glorious opportunities. He is preparing you for the glory of His Kingdom.

God, I'm not into pain, but I'm into You. And I'll trust You to lead me through every difficult situation I encounter into wonderful things ahead.

day 198

Rejoice that you participate in the sufferings of Christ, so that you may be overjoyed when his glory is revealed.
1 Peter 4:13 NIV

Redemptive Pain

Everyone on planet Earth gets to experience pain. It's part of a fallen world, a world twisted by sin. So the only choice you really get is this: Will your pain be pointless or redemptive?

One of King Solomon's favorite images in the book of Proverbs is the crucible—the place where precious metal is heated and refined. The refining, or redemption, of these metals required a sufficient amount of heat to purge the impurities. When you trust the heart of God toward you, you can receive pain in similar fashion. It is the kindness of God that reveals the flaws and impurities of your own soul so that you can die to self and live to God.

The New Rebellion is a call to glorious things in the Kingdom. It's also a call to join the sufferings of Christ.

I'm willing to walk with You, God, through places dark and difficult. Use every hardship and place of suffering to make me more like You.

day 199

"The LORD gave and the LORD has taken away; may the name of the LORD be praised." In all this, Job did not sin by charging God with wrongdoing.
Job 1:21–22 NIV

Ruthless Trust

Job had it harder than anyone else. He lost almost everything he held dear—his possessions, his children, his health, his future. He even lost the affections and support of his wife. He lost the confidence of his closest friends. In a very brief amount of time, Job went from the pinnacle of esteem in his community to the depths of humiliation. However tough you've had it, Job probably has you beat.

And although this man of suffering struggled through bitterness of soul, he continued to honor God, and God affirmed the integrity of his heart. Even while Job was tossed and torn by grief and confusion, his anchoring conviction that God was God would not be dislodged. He knew to whom he belonged and trusted Him ruthlessly even as he wrestled against the injustice he felt. Pain brought him to worship.

This day, O God, anchor my heart forever in You.
No matter what I face, help me trust You even when
I don't understand You.

day 200

It is commendable if a man bears up under the pain of unjust suffering because he is conscious of God.
1 Peter 2:19 NIV

True Grit

John Wayne wasn't exactly the model of Christian virtue. While full of noble intentions, his characters were entirely self-sufficient; they didn't usually experience much in terms of true community. He wasn't a big communicator. But he had one thing: He had true grit. He was tough. And toughness counts for something in this world.

It's not the kind of toughness that makes you calloused, cynical, and unfeeling. God's vision of toughness is men and women who have suffered and don't quit. In this letter, the apostle Peter notes that suffering unjustly brings commendation. If you earn your sufferings through foolishness—as all do from time to time—well, that's not very special. But those who persevere through undeserved pain and keep their hearts tender and open are those counted great in the Kingdom.

Increase my "grit," God. Give me a tenaciousness of soul that can survive and even thrive when others lose heart. Keep me conscious of You!

day 201

He was despised and rejected—a man of sorrows, acquainted with bitterest grief.
Isaiah 53:3 NLT

Imitation Is the Sincerest Flattery

Jesus did not choose the pain that dogged His days of ministry and eventually took His life. But neither did He run from it. Instead, He held the course that was His authentic destiny from the Father and let the chips fall where they may. Jesus' course led Him through great suffering and out again into the glory and satisfaction of His Father's arms.

Your life has a model. Your life has a mentor, and His name is Jesus. If you'll fix your attention on Him, He will tell you your destiny. Not only that, He'll lead you into it, through it, and out the other side. Don't choose your course on the presence or absence of pain but on the whispers of heaven. When you do, heaven itself will sustain you through pain and reward you on the other side.

I want the course You destined me for, God. None other!
I want to follow You through blessings and
hardships into Your arms.

day 202

If one member suffers, all the members suffer with it.
1 Corinthians 12:26 HCSB

Dividing the Sorrows

Paul's analogy of God's people as a "body" is brilliant. The essential connectedness of it, the interdependency, the mutuality—it aptly conveys that your life is not your own; you are organically bound up in the form and function, the beauty and the destiny, of every other child of God. There's no getting away from it!

This revelation requires a substantial amount of compassion and care toward one another, because in this sense to love one another is to love one's own "body," one's own self. Your pain radiates across all those whose lives are joined to yours. And their sufferings affect you as well. In this way, God's people bear one another's sorrows. They strengthen, encourage, and refocus their brothers and sisters. This may be part of your Kingdom calling today—if you have eyes to see and a heart to empower.

God, help me get beyond myself to be a restorer of others. Activate my faith to renew the hearts of those who need You today.

day 203

Whenever a woman is in labor she has pain . . . but when she gives birth to the child, she no longer remembers the anguish because of the joy . . . you too have grief now; but I will see you again, and your heart will rejoice.
John 16:21–22 NASB

Surprised by Joy

You are destined for joy, and not just in heaven! God intends to show His goodness in your life in a multitude of ways right here in this world. The book of Galatians reminds you that joy is an evidence (fruit) of the Spirit's presence inside your heart, so you can expect Him to lace your days with the pleasure of His nearness. This is your rightful inheritance as a child of God.

However, joy is frequently blended with pain. Occasionally, pain is just to be endured. Usually, pain is a tool of growth. And sometimes, pain is actually the vehicle for birthing something wonderful—a vision, a relationship, a ministry, or a Kingdom future. God doesn't waste pain, so don't you waste it either. Look carefully for the joy that emerges after the hard and difficult times.

God, I'm taking hold of faith today that the difficulties in my life will actually be the conduit for blessing and purpose.

day 204

Every good and perfect gift is from above, coming down from the Father of the heavenly lights, who does not change like shifting shadows.
James 1:17 NIV

Immutability—Always Consistent

When it comes to understanding God, square one is comprehending His unceasing goodness. Everything else in your life may shift and dance like shadows in candlelight—but not God! Even your closest friends and family will fail you from time to time, but God is utterly reliable in your life and in the world.

The world is crying out for something true, someone dependable. Every soul longs for a place of security and is usually disappointed. But God cannot exist apart from His character; He is defined by absolute consistency combined with absolute goodness.

The New Rebellion will live out the reckless joy and inner brilliance of this unshakable foundation. And as your life reflects this larger reality, it will confront the pervasive cynicism of contemporary culture—and rekindle the hope of all seekers.

You are my "good and perfect gift," God, and I find unceasing hope and confidence in Your commitment to me!

God is not a man, that He should lie, nor a son of man, that He should repent; has He said, and will He not do it? Or has He spoken, and will He not make it good?
Numbers 23:19 NASB

day 205

Veracity—Always True

God's words, like His character, are completely trustworthy. The Bible, unique among all religious writings, contains more than two thousand prophecies that have already been fulfilled. Now that's reliability! More to the point, His promises will always be true *to you*. The how's and when's of His delivery are up to Him—and frequently perplexing to His children. But He always comes through.

Your challenge is to represent a God of uncompromising trustworthiness through the conduct of your life. Do your choices, conversation, and behavior proclaim an unwavering confidence in God's truthfulness? Does your own character reflect that godly quality—not in perfection but as characteristic—and instill confidence in those who know you?

It's okay to question God, to wrestle with Him, to confess your doubts. But at the end of the day, you know in your heart of hearts that He will always come through for you.

Today I trust You with my life and with my world, God. I will never allow my confusion to call Your character into question.

day 206

I am God, and there is no one else like me. Only I can tell you what is going to happen even before it happens. Everything I plan will come to pass, for I do whatever I wish.
Isaiah 46:9–10 NLT

Omniscience—Always Knowing

The awareness that God knows the most minute of information about you—your thoughts and imaginations, your fantasies and dreams—not to mention about every other soul on the planet, inspires both awe and security in the hearts of God's children.

Adam and Eve's choice to distrust God and then disobey Him activated a primal urge to hide. But God's great love could not be shaken so easily. His knowledge of your soul—the good, the bad, and the ugly—doesn't distance Him from you. It simply fuels His outrageous passion for you and for His good destiny in your life.

The New Rebellion consists of men and women who live in the absolute security of a God who knows all things and directs all things according to His own good design. You're a Rebel with a cause.

God, I welcome Your intimate knowledge of me, and I want to know You with equal intimacy, knowing that nothing can separate me from Your love.

day 207

Is there anyplace I can go to avoid your Spirit? To be out of your sight? If I climb to the sky, you're there! If I go underground, you're there!
Psalm 139:7–8 MSG

Omnipresence—Always There

Why would you ever want to get away from God? He's the safest, best answer to a crazy world . . . the truest part of a false world . . . the only source of unconditional love in a very conditional world. You can't get away, and nothing else can tear you away either. It's the best "good news" ever!

But the very truth that wraps your soul in the sweet scent of possession threatens many others. God's pervasive presence holds all men and women accountable for their actions—a very unpleasant thought for those who reject His lordship in their lives. And so your presence, as a representative of the divine presence, will bring life to some and death to others.

You never have to try to hold people accountable—that's the Holy Spirit's job. Your job is to know God and let Him live His life through you. It's very simple, and it is transformingly powerful in the earth.

Thank You, God for being the air I breathe, the sun I feel, the road I walk, and for constantly surrounding my life with love and purpose.

day
208

"Nothing will be impossible with God." "I am the Lord's slave," said Mary. "May it be done to me according to your word."
Luke 1:37–38 HCSB

Omnipotence—Always in Charge

All-knowing. Ever-present. And all-powerful. There is nothing and no one who can challenge the authority of God. The devil, who has been given a small measure of authority, works his best to "steal, kill, and destroy" (see John 10:10). But he is powerless to resist the march of God's will across the plains of time.

Mary recognized this in her own life—that she served the God of the impossible. And so do you! You must understand this in order to move in the New Rebellion. You must walk in the expectation that God intends to do impossible things through your life, things you could never accomplish in your own ability, things that will bring honor and attention to Him alone.

This is the power of God's omnipotence in the life of a Christ-follower. His authority operates in and through you.

God, like Mary I say, "I am Your servant. Do everything You want to do in my life, and make me a conduit for Your power and purpose."

Know therefore that the LORD your God is God; he is the faithful God, keeping his covenant of love to a thousand generations of those who love him and keep his commands.
Deuteronomy 7:9 NIV

day 209

Always Faithful

God's commitment to your life just will not quit. There is no promise from Him that will not be fulfilled, no heavenly passion for you that will ever fade from His eyes, and no destiny for your life that He will abandon!

God's not like us. He doesn't forget, doesn't give up, doesn't change His mind. He is 100 percent faithful to His goodness in your life. Today may hold disappointments, unexpected turns of events, even tragedy for someone. But God's power brings beauty out of ashes, and the broken places of your life are the seedbed of hope and delight. This is the kind of God you serve.

As the disciple Peter once said, "Lord, to whom shall we go? You have the words of eternal life" (John 6:68 NIV).

God, there's no one like You, no one else who is utterly trustworthy in this world. Help me to be as faithful to You as You are to me.

day 210

One thing God has spoken, two things have I heard: that you, O God, are strong, and that you, O Lord, are loving. Surely you will reward each person according to what he has done.
Psalm 62:11–12 NIV

Strong but Always Compassionate

This verse brings together two of God's greatest attributes: His power and His love. David found through his circumstances that these two qualities in God were the foundation of his life—the glasses through which he made sense of his world.

If God is good, and He is, then you can always trust His intentions and activity in your life. You can go through any difficulty if you truly believe that all things are working together for good, that every event is a vehicle for God to establish His goodness in and through you.

If God is strong, and He is, then you know He is able to enforce His good intentions in your life. Nothing can prevent His purposes from coming into reality for you. This is the foundation for your world and calling in the New Rebellion.

I dedicate my life to the exploration of Your goodness and power in the world. And I expect You to be good and strong for me today.

If anyone is a hearer of the word and not a doer, he is like a man looking at his own face in a mirror; for he looks at himself, goes away, and right away forgets what kind of man he was.
James 1:23–24 HCSB

day 211

Absentminded

The scenario may sound a bit absurd—how can someone forget his own face?! But it can be a pretty accurate picture when it comes to your life in God.

Obedience to God's Word means many things. It means following the commands of Scripture. But it's more than that. God's Word is a window to His character. Your obedience to that Word includes living in the conscious reality of God's character.

It's all too easy to forget what God has done in your past: the deliverances, the provision, the direction, the comfort. Your history in God is meant to become the supporting fabric that undergirds your soul in dark times. The remembrance of how God demonstrated His character in other places and seasons is an extremely potent weapon against your enemy's efforts to discourage and distract you today. Do you see that?

Help me remember Your ways and Your works in my history, God. I don't want to lose the heritage You have given me.

Remembrance

day
212

Thus Joash the king did not remember the kindness
which Jehoiada his father had done to him,
but killed his son.
2 Chronicles 24:22 NKJV

The Consequences of Forgetfulness

Forgetfulness is not without its consequences. The history of Israel is one continuous case study in the results of forgetfulness. Because each current generation rarely passed their experience and convictions along to the upcoming generation, their children would cease to obey God and find themselves in terrible conditions as a result.

The primary results of forgetfulness are self-sufficiency and hardness of heart. Do you find those dynamics creeping into your soul? The antidote is remembrance—go back and rehearse the works of God in your past. If you are a second-generation Christian, dig into the faith stories of your parents or grandparents. Find out how your story is connected to the larger story of your family line. And then take hold of God's character and purpose for you today.

God, help me to learn from the mistakes of others and to not have to repeat them; help me to renew Your faithfulness in my memory.

day 213

Mary treasured all these things, pondering them in her heart . . . and His mother treasured all these things in her heart.
Luke 2:19, 51 NASB

Unexpected Treasure

When the words and deeds of God are remembered and pondered and meditated upon over time, an amazing thing happens: They become a treasure supply—a reservoir of illumination into the heart of the Father. Mary's treasure sustained her during some very dark times, the darkest times a mother can experience.

But did you know that Mary's treasure can be yours? You, too, can store up your encounters with God; you, too, can study and reflect upon the meaning of the events in your life. These ponderings will become a source of spiritual insight and divine relationship that will empower your destiny.

Those who remember what God says and does become able communicators of God to their world. Spread the wealth! Invest your heart in remembering; then you'll be able to speak for God with conviction.

I set my will to remember God's words and treasure them up in my heart so that I can convey His heart to my world.

day
214

Taking bread, he blessed it, broke it, and gave it to them; saying, "This is my body, given for you. Eat it in my memory." He did the same with the cup after supper, saying, "This cup is the new covenant written in my blood, blood poured out for you."
Luke 22:19–20 MSG

Empowering Remembrance

Among all the commands of Christ, there is one that sticks out: when Jesus urged His disciples to eat bread and drink wine as a way of remembering His very own body and blood, the sacrifice for redeeming God's children. Communion is not just a Christian ritual or ceremony. It's all about stirring up your mind and your passion by replaying the life and death of Jesus on the vivid inner screen of your imagination.

To remember Christ in this way is to encounter and renew the power of God's life within you. It is a very real and intimate avenue between you and heaven. And in this way, spiritual remembrance fuels the New Rebellion. Your meditation upon Jesus' life and death prepares you like little else to live and eventually to die as He did: loving people into the Kingdom.

God, whether my remembrance is formalized in Communion or as informal as my own thoughts, I want Your life to be the center of my day.

day 215

He who sacrifices thank offerings honors me,
and he prepares the way so that I may
show him the salvation of God.
Psalm 50:23 NIV

A Potent Gratitude

Remembering the times and ways God has invaded your world with His love and power is like puncturing an aerosol can—the thankfulness just starts busting out all over the place! There's just no other response that makes sense like gratitude! Which is simply another name for worship.

When you tap the thanksgiving that's inside you, you are bringing God what He most deserves: honor. This one thing is the most right thing in the world! And when the glory of God is amplified through your thanks, something else happens. You open the door for God to break into your world yet again with delivering power. So, if you're facing some tough enemies, just begin to praise God; before you know it, angels will be en route to break your situation open and set you free!

Remind me today, God, when situations turn impossible to release all my gratitude to You in worship and thanksgiving. I'm ready for Your deliverance!

day 216

Tie them to your hands as a reminder, and wear them on your forehead. Write them on the doorposts of your house and on your gates.
Deuteronomy 6:8–9 NLT

Whatever It Takes!

The Law of God that Moses brought to the people of Israel contained many vivid physical practices that reinforced the concepts that were most dear to God's heart. And since one of God's passions is to have His ways remembered and not forgotten, He designed some unusual ways of helping the Jews remember.

He told them to write down His laws and then tie those papers onto their bodies! To tie His revelations to their hands and their foreheads. Wow! That's radical. God must think this memory stuff is pretty important! Then He told them to write His commands on their door frames and gates. God's words would be in their face. They would be constantly reminded of God's character and their identity. And though these specific forms no longer apply to those in the covenant of grace, the reality they represent will always be important to God.

God, I'm going to put Your Word before my eyes
in lots of creative ways. Teach me to love
Your ways more and more.

day 217

I will remember the deeds of the LORD; yes, I will remember your miracles of long ago. I will meditate on all your works and consider all your mighty deeds.
Psalm 77:11–12 NIV

Remembrance Is Worship

Remembrance involves bringing back to your mind the things God has done in your life. Even the things He's done for others—maybe others in your family or others in the Bible. But it doesn't stop there. Then you meditate on them. You consider the meaning of what God has done. You mull over why God does what He does—how His actions convey His values and how His values have an impact on your world.

But it doesn't stop there either. Giving this level of attention to God and His ways is essentially an act of worship. It is remembering for the purpose of honoring. And when you tell others what God has done in your life, then you are completing the cycle—you are praising the person and acts of God. And you are training your heart in His ways.

You are beyond amazing, God! Your wisdom blows my mind. Your kindness shatters my imagination. I'll never stop pondering Your goodness.

day 218

You will make known to me the path of life; in Your presence is fullness of joy; in Your right hand there are pleasures forever.
Psalm 16:11 NASB

Christian Hedonism

A pastor named John Piper coined the provocative phrase "Christian hedonism" to describe God's compelling desire to bring the greatest joy possible into the lives of His children. The fact that this world is rife with pain and difficulty does not diminish God's intent or your destiny. You are designed for joy. Heaven will be the greatest expression of that joy—a joy that increases exponentially for eternity—but in the meantime, the New Rebellion is about the business of bringing heaven to earth!

The presence of God is "joy inexpressible and full of joy" (1 Peter 1:8 NKJV). Where God is, there is joy. Even in the midst of loss. The beauty of God and His redemptive lovingkindness overshadow every brand of suffering. Your assignment is to live in that presence and bring its pleasures into your world.

God, I want my life to be forever marked by the joy of Your presence. Cause me to live in that reality all twenty-four hours today.

For seven days celebrate the Feast to the LORD your God at the place the LORD will choose. For the LORD your God will bless you in all your harvest and in all the work of your hands, and your joy will be complete.
Deuteronomy 16:15 NIV

day 219

A Generous Joy

It is vital to your effectiveness as a Kingdom Rebel to know and demonstrate the character of the God you serve. And one of the central facets of God's character is His generosity. Those who focus on the commandments of God without seeing them in the context of His lavish loving-kindness become tight-lipped, white-knuckled legalists like the Pharisees.

While there are seasons of sacrifice and hard work, they are meant to be followed by joy and celebration, by feasting and abundance. The heart of God is most accurately revealed in blessing and intimacy . . . which means that your character and behavior must reflect the same if you intend to represent the Kingdom on earth. Seek a lifestyle of generosity with all you possess—kindness, money, affirmation, serving. Resist the urge to hoard your possessions or be stingy with those in need.

God, let the quality of my generosity mirror the beauty of heaven and spread the joys of heaven everywhere I go.

day 220

What happens when we live God's way? He brings gifts into our lives, much the same way that fruit appears in an orchard—things like affection for others, exuberance about life, serenity.
Galatians 5:22 MSG

Exuberance

The thing about plants and harvest is that their fruit indicates two things: identity and resource. If a tree in an orchard begins to grow round, orange objects that look like oranges and smell like oranges and taste like oranges . . . then it's probably an orange tree. And whether that orange tree produces a handful of shriveled oranges or hundreds of ripe, luscious oranges probably reflects the amount of water, sunlight, and soil nutrition that is available.

Your life will also produce fruit in accordance with its design and nourishment. If your life springs from the "seed" of God's Kingdom, then you are going to develop the characteristics of the Kingdom. The abundance of your soul is meant to channel God's care of you into rich fruit that brings great joy to others. That they can taste and exuberantly delight in.

I want to spread joy, God. Lots of it and in
lots of places! I want to be so full that
Your goodness pours out everywhere.

day 221

The Seventy returned with joy, saying, "Lord, even the demons submit to us in Your name."
Luke 10:17 HCSB

Doin' the Stuff

When seventy of Jesus' disciples were sent out with His authority to do His will, they began to operate in the power of heaven—a power that broke demonic authority off people's lives and released them into the freedom of salvation. To observe such liberation and, more than that, to be the vehicle of such liberation elicited a passionate joy in these men and women. And this is God's desire for your life as well.

You get to "do the stuff" of the gospel! You're not just a bystander. You're not just warming the bench; you're a player. And as such, you get to participate in all the joy of your heavenly Coach. Today, look for God to release you redemptively into the lives of others. Enjoy it. It's God's gift to you . . . and them.

*God, let Your joy for me flow out of Your power in my life.
Make me an avenue of Your healing
authority in the world today.*

day 222

What has happened to all your joy? . . . Have I now become your enemy by telling you the truth?
Galatians 4:15–16 NIV

Losing Joy

Because joy is a key evidence of the Kingdom's activity in your life, the absence of joy should raise a serious red flag and tell you something isn't right. The lack of joy needs to trigger a response from you—a motivation to find whatever's wrong and fix it!

Paul noticed that the Christians in Galatia had lost their joy. In this case, it was the result of leaving the freedom of God's grace and trying once again to earn God's favor by their own self-effort. And nothing will kill joy faster than that deception. He says that it's tantamount to going back into slavery again. So Paul gets in their face and risks inciting their anger by confronting them with their mistake. He is zealous to see their joy renewed. Protect your own joy . . . and that of other believers.

God, keep me right smack in the middle of Your empowering grace and the joy that comes with Your freedom from sin and self-effort.

Restore to me again the joy of your salvation,
and make me willing to obey you.
Psalm 51:12 NLT

Renewed Joy

This poignant psalm was penned by King David immediately following his great sin—a terrible combination of adultery and murder. Needless to say, David lost his joy! The guilt of his wrongdoing overwhelmed him and blotted out the inner life and joy he had carefully cultivated for so many years. His commitment to the Kingdom had earned him the description of "a man after God's own heart"! But now the joy of that fellowship was gone.

Fortunately, David knew the power of God's redemption—a life that overcomes the power of death and sin. In the agony of humility, he cried out for cleansing and forgiveness . . . and received that precious gift. When guilt threatens your joy, run once again to the fountain of freedom and find the restoration of fellowship and joy that belongs to you.

God, I will never let sin own me. As soon as I see it, I will run to You and renew the joy of my salvation.

day 224

Do not sorrow, for the joy of the LORD is your strength.
Nehemiah 8:10 NKJV

Joy Has Muscles

While you're engaged in the Rebellion, you will face times of sorrow and sadness. There will be moments when strength is gone, and you don't want to face another day. In the midst of this challenge, God remains your source. And a mighty weapon against doubt and discouragement is the gift of joy.

Joy is not merely the result of God's presence. Joy can often be the bringer of God's presence. And in this sense, joy is a skill to be cultivated and developed. You can choose to move in joy, even when you don't feel it. It's not wishful thinking: It's simply aligning yourself with the truth of God's realm. It's acknowledging who you are and who God is. That is joy! And when you take hold of it, the very strength of heaven is released within you.

Help me to remember who I am, God,
and to reach down deep for the joy
of being Your son or daughter.

Do you not know that those who run in a race all run, but only one receives the prize? Run in such a way that you may win. Everyone who competes in the games exercises self-control in all things. They then do it to receive a perishable wreath, but we an imperishable.
1 Corinthians 9:24–25 NASB

day 225

Spring Training

The Kingdom race is not a competition among one another; however, your race is contested by spiritual enemies who want to distract you, slow you down, and get you off course. It's sort of like running a marathon through a war zone! You can't let down your guard or get lazy. Your life, and the lives of others, depends upon your ability to be self-controlled, to stay focused, and to run with perseverance.

This kind of personal discipline requires training—it means you don't eat spiritual "junk food." This might mean elevating the standards for the movies, books, and music you feed your soul. It might mean that you exercise your spirit through classic practices like prayer, meditation, solitude, and study of God's Word. It's not about earning God's favor; it's about getting equipped for Kingdom effectiveness.

Train me, God. Equip me. Teach me how to run straight for heaven's prize and not be hindered or distracted by lesser things.

day 226

Whoever has no rule over his own spirit is like a city broken down, without walls.
Proverbs 25:28 NKJV

Defenseless!

Self-control is a vital quality for the women and men of the New Rebellion. Proverbs says that the lack of it is equivalent to having no walls of protection around the "city" of your life! In other words, those who cannot control their attitudes, motivations, and actions are sitting ducks for spiritual enemies. Without spiritual discipline, you'll be invaded by whatever feelings or lies the enemy throws at you and unable to defend yourself with truth and power.

With self-control, it's important to understand that self is the object being controlled, not the subject doing the controlling. The strength to defend your life comes not from you, but from the Holy Spirit. He is the One who means to control your heart and your behavior. And when you submit to His control, you find great protection.

Be the wall that surrounds my life, God. Control every part of me so that I'm defended and empowered by heaven itself.

Knowing God leads to self-control. Self-control leads to patient endurance, and patient endurance leads to godliness.
2 Peter 1:6 NLT

day 227

The Missing Link

Every Kingdom Rebel wants to both know God and become more like God—to be formed in character to more accurately reflect the glory of God. This is part of your destiny and essential purpose. But sometimes the gap between knowing God and being formed into His image is large. The missing link is self-control. Here's how it works.

Knowing God is not so much about obtaining knowledge as it is about allowing Him to be Lord of your life, allowing God's Spirit to lead you, inform you, direct you, and use you. The more you take your own hands off the steering wheel of your life, the more you learn to endure difficulties and tests with patience. Why? Because you trust Him. And in the process, your character is transformed day by day to be more like His!

God, I want to get hooked up with You. I want to know You deeply and truly and to be like You in every way possible.

day 228

Roll up your sleeves, put your mind in gear, be totally ready to receive the gift that's coming when Jesus arrives. Don't lazily slip back into those old grooves of evil, doing just what you feel like doing.
1 Peter 1:13–14 MSG

Armed and Dangerous

Self-control keeps you focused. It affirms both your identity and your purpose. It arms you for action that is consistent with your calling as a Rebel of the Kingdom.

There is a constant though subtle pressure to slack off the pursuit of God and His interests; there is a dulling influence from your spiritual enemy that wants to lull you back into the "old grooves of evil." But when your "self" is controlled by the Spirit, your heart remains engaged in your true passion and you become dangerous to this world's system!

This is no time to be stuck in idle. You have one life to live—stay in gear, moving in godly ways toward godly objectives. In this way, you won't be ashamed when Jesus returns; in fact, your joy will be complete because you have held the course.

Keep me engaged, God, with the relationships and activities that are essential to my calling. Don't let me get distracted and pulled off course.

day 229

The fear of the LORD is the beginning of knowledge,
but fools despise wisdom and discipline.
Proverbs 1:7 NIV

The Headwaters

The fear of the Lord is a strange paradox. Why would anyone be afraid of the sum total of all goodness in the universe? In short, because real goodness is somewhat terrifying. We call it holiness, and although it promises you absolute kindness, it also holds you absolutely accountable for every action . . . even the secret ones. Those who embrace this dangerous holiness of God, with both its risks and rewards, discover the source of true knowledge and begin to learn His good ways.

Discipline, or self-control, is the natural by-product of this holy fear, this reverence and awe for God's rule. It moves you to align yourself with who He is and what He's doing in the earth. It constrains you from foolish choices and motivates you to pursue what is noble and righteous in your world.

Be the source, the headwaters of all that is good in me, God.
Teach me the wonderful fear of You that draws
me close to Your heart.

day 230

Submit to God. But resist the Devil, and he will flee from you.
James 4:7 HCSB

Double Duty

The Spirit-controlled self will always be led to two simultaneous activities—submitting joyfully and expectantly to the will of God and at the same time resisting the will of the devil. While the same activity may accomplish both objectives, it is important to remain conscious of each.

Resisting the devil takes many forms. Sometimes he is obvious; more often he is sneaky. Sometimes his will emerges out of your own selfishness or misdirected desires—biblically, this is called "the flesh." Sometimes you feel pressure from the motivations and values of this world's system. Sometimes you are harassed directly by evil spirits. The self-controlled man or woman resists, submits to God, and their enemy will flee. He must! He cannot stand before the will of God, and when you are lined up with God, he can't stand against you either.

God, I am so happy to submit myself to You today. Take my will and mold it to Yours. Then I will stand against my enemy.

day
231

Since we belong to the day, let us be self-controlled,
putting on faith and love as a breastplate,
and the hope of salvation as a helmet.
1 Thessalonians 5:8 NIV

This Is War

You belong to the day. You belong to Jesus and are a warrior for His Kingdom in this world. This is your identity, your security, and your destiny! Own that reality today.

Now, possessing that identity, step into a Spirit-controlled life today. He is your coach and commander. Not only do you belong to Him, but you are safe with Him. Abandon yourself to His good direction. Now, as a warrior, it's time to put on your armor—love defines your heart; faith protects your heart. The hope of your salvation (your confidence in God's ownership) protects your mind.

Now, expect God to lead you into this day as a world-changer. You will confront spiritual enemies today . . . and win! You will be a breath of freedom and hope to others who are struggling. You will bring blessing wherever you go.

God, I'm ready to fight the good fight of faith today.
Strengthen me and lead me and be my joy in the journey!

day 232

Praise be to the God and Father of our Lord Jesus Christ, the Father of compassion and the God of all comfort, who comforts us in all our troubles, so that we can comfort those in any trouble with the comfort we ourselves have received from God.
2 Corinthians 1:3–4 NIV

The Source

As a Kingdom Rebel, it's not enough to know the truth. People can be bludgeoned by truth, but that was not the way Jesus moved throughout the earth. Jesus' ministry was consistently marked by love and compassion . . . and yours must be as well. As the old saying goes, "People don't care how much you know until they know how much you care!"

God's intent for your life is to be a channel of comfort and compassion—receiving deeply for your own needs and then giving out generously to others. What qualifies you to minister to others is having received that same ministry from God yourself. It may flow directly from His Spirit or it may come to you through other Kingdom Rebels. Trouble is a mainstay in a fallen world, so you will have unending opportunity to care for others with compassion.

Thank You for Your kindness and compassion that is so rich to me, God. Now help me be a source of Your care for others.

day
233

You, O Lord, are a compassionate and gracious God,
slow to anger, abounding in love and faithfulness.
Psalm 86:15 NIV

Compassionate When It Costs

Compassion does have a price tag attached.

Can you care for people who hurt you? Can you look beyond people's obnoxiousness or selfishness and see their needs? Can you see where they have been hurt and then act out their hurt again toward others in a multiplication of sin? Now, can you see the grace of God that cuts the root of sin and alienation and brings healing to wounded people?

If you can see these things, then you are beginning to look at the world through the Father's eyes. You are beginning to see redemptively and to move restoratively. You are most like Christ when you overlook personal injury and offense, resist the invitation to anger, and then reach out in grace and compassion to heal. Love looks past the cost to the opportunity.

Give me Your perspective, God, so that I can see what You want to do in other people and then partner with You in their healing.

day 234

Mercy and truth have met together;
righteousness and peace have kissed.
Psalm 85:10 NKJV

Balancing a Bike

God has a way of winding up in the middle of many paradoxes. In other words, ideas that seem to oppose one another find their unity in God. One person likens it to pedaling a bicycle. If you push down on one pedal, the opposite pedal rises up; if you push down on that one, the other immediately raises its head. It's an interesting picture.

The opposite concepts of mercy and truth are largely that way. Truth and justice can sometimes feel harsh and demanding even while you recognize their importance. Mercy and compassion can sometimes feel licentious, lacking integrity. But in Christ both of these Kingdom values come together in a wonderful balance. By giving each "pedal" its appropriate attention, the Kingdom moves forward with purpose and momentum. And the result is as beautiful as a kiss.

Bring me into that same balance, God, where both discernment and compassion flow freely from my life to the nourishment of others.

day 235

You're blessed when you care. At the moment of being "care-full," you find yourselves cared for.
Matthew 5:7 MSG

Reciprocity

On day one this week, you looked at how being able to receive God's care enables you to turn around and give that same care back to other people. That is a powerful truth. But the cycle doesn't stop there; it continues to perpetuate itself. When you give compassionate care to others, you also generate a blessing back toward yourself: You find God raising up other folks who will care for you in return.

Neither sin nor righteousness exists as an individual act. Each one generates a return on investment—sin has a way of generating more sin, both to others and back on yourself. But fortunately, compassion generates even more. In fact, God says that sin affects people three or four generations removed from you but that compassion lasts for a thousand generations!

God, I want to unleash a tsunami of love and compassion that will reciprocate to me but also affect others for generations to come.

day 236

Let him who boasts boast of this, that he understands and knows me, that I am the LORD who exercises lovingkindness, justice and righteousness on earth; for I delight in these things.
Jeremiah 9:24 NASB

The Fellowship of Compassion

You can't claim to know God while failing to understand His essential commitment to loving-kindness in the earth. His compassion exists harmoniously alongside His justice and righteousness—together they reflect His character. God takes great joy and delight in the way these three elements work together, and if you want to know God, then you need to develop a deep appreciation for all three.

As your life begins to take on the shape of God's agenda, it begins to unlock a very special dynamic: a fellowship between you and God! This is beyond salvation, or, perhaps more accurately stated, a continuation of salvation. It's a dynamic that moves us from being children of God to being partners with God in the world. Partnership implies a very intimate fellowship, but it can't happen until you understand God's motivations.

Teach me more, God, about Your passion for compassion
and how that fits with Your justice and righteousness.
I want to understand Your heart.

day 237

"The LORD bless him!" Naomi said to her daughter-in-law. "He has not stopped showing his kindness to the living and the dead."
Ruth 2:20 NIV

Compassion Affects Destiny

Ruth was a godly young woman in Israel long ago, a woman absolutely impoverished. In those times, women without other means of support would walk through harvested fields of grain to pick up the leftovers. In Ruth's case, she found compassion from a landowner named Boaz, who offered her protection and extra grain. Because his character reflected the compassion of God, it opened a door to destiny—the door to his marriage of Ruth and becoming the great-grandfather of King David and, eventually, Jesus Himself.

Compassion opens up avenues for the purpose of God in your life. When you move in God's character, you begin to reap God's reward—the life you were created for. How might God use you today to amplify His expressions of kindness to those you touch? Will you open up doors of destiny for them?

Here I am, God. Release Your loving compassion in my soul—let me feel what You feel and open up Kingdom opportunities today.

day 238

I have compassion on the crowd, because they've
already stayed with Me three days
and have nothing to eat.
Mark 8:2 HCSB

Compassion Opens the Door to Miracles

Jesus' compassion opened windows of opportunity for Him constantly. They allowed Jesus to be an avenue of blessing wherever He went, and one avenue of blessing was the miraculous flow of healing and other miracles. In this case, it was a miraculous dinner. But it was also more than that—even as He filled people's stomachs, He opened their eyes to the nature of God and His destiny over their lives.

Miracles are a powerful wake-up call! They bring an invasion of an infinite heaven into the earthiness of a very finite world. God uses them to awaken people to Kingdom realities that are often cloaked by the busyness of the ordinary. Through miracles, He enables ordinary men and women to live extraordinary lives of significance and power just like yours! Are you ready to have Him work miracles through you?

I'm ready, God. Release Your Kingdom authority inside and through my life to bring Your purposes on the earth! And please start today.

Don't burn out; keep yourselves fueled and aflame. Be alert servants of the Master, cheerfully expectant. Don't quit in hard times; pray all the harder. Help needy Christians; be inventive in hospitality.
Romans 12:11–13 MSG

day 239

Short, Sweet, and to the Point

The New Rebellion is about serving others in love. Jesus was foremost a servant while He walked our earth, looking for ways to help people in need. Your mission in life is to be alert servants, always ready to give something of yourself to other people.

This verse urges you not to quit in hard times, but to never cease caring for others in creative ways. Sometimes life has a way of grabbing your attention—pain, fear, grief—these are things that can tackle you and rub the dirt of life in your face so that you get choked up with your own problems. When this happens, you have to get "fueled" up with God's Spirit so you can give your attention again to others. Recharged by God, you will avoid burnout, and be ready to serve those God brings into your world.

God, You are such a good example of helping people. I want to bring life into other people's lives—teach me how to do this.

day 240

Bless the LORD, all you His hosts, you who serve Him, doing His will. Bless the LORD, all you works of His, in all places of His dominion; bless the LORD, O my soul!
Psalm 103:21–22 NASB

The Heart of the Kingdom

The call of the Kingdom—"Follow Me!"—is a call to follow in the footsteps of Christ as a servant. Jesus came to serve those who were desperate in body, mind, and spirit and to invite you into serving alongside Him. It's not optional. But neither is it drudgery.

The call to serve God, and those God leads you to, could be seen as slavish. In truth, the apostles embraced, rather than shunned, the concept of being a slave for Christ. But in the heart of God, serving is always the pathway to true freedom. Neither can serving God be separated from your worship of God, as this passage illuminates! Blessing the Lord with your mouth is organically connected to serving Him with your feet. They are, in fact, one and the same action—simply expressed in two different, but essential, manifestations.

God, let the praises of my mouth be consistent with the love that flows from my life in serving others practically.

day 241

You are called to freedom, brothers; only don't use this freedom as an opportunity for the flesh, but serve one another through love.
Galatians 5:13 HCSB

It's Not About You

Freedom of soul is the one thing every human heart most longs for and most needs. To be free from addictions, wrong motivations, lying, fear—among all the many enslavements of this planet—is the fragrance of heaven on earth. It is the redemption of sin's curse that first subjugated Adam and Eve so long ago.

Jesus purchased your freedom through an extreme servanthood, submission to a brutal death by crucifixion. He served you through His love to empower you to serve others through that same heavenly love. Your liberation from the tyranny of sin enables you to love like there's no tomorrow! Now you're free. Now you can love and serve through the power of the Cross.

Serving flows naturally from a ransomed heart. The motivation of love and gratitude moves you to give others what's been given to you.

God, thank You for being the ultimate servant and setting my longing heart free. Help me today to serve powerfully and expansively.

day 242

Each one should use whatever gift he has received to serve others, faithfully administering God's grace in its various forms.
1 Peter 4:10 NIV

Power Serve

One definition of grace is the power to be the real you in the real world.

This power to live true to your heavenly calling comes only from heaven, but God intends to use His sons and daughters as conduits of that heavenly grace through their spiritual gifts. The New Rebellion depends upon it. Aren't you glad that God has given you unique ways to express His powerful grace? They're not meant to keep for yourself and use on yourself; you are meant to live for the good of others. This is the real you.

A proverb says, "Your own soul is nourished when you are kind" (11:17 NLT); in other words, when you use your gifts for the good of others you are also being kind to yourself. What's more, you are faithfully stewarding the grace God has entrusted to you.

God, Your gifts are so good, Your grace so empowering. Allow me to serve others well this day through the gifts You've given me.

In pointing out these things to the brethren, you will be a good servant of Christ Jesus, constantly nourished on the words of the faith and of the sound doctrine which you have been following.
1 Timothy 4:6 NASB

day 243

Emotional Equilibrium

Have you ever considered that one way you can serve your brothers and sisters in Christ is by pointing out where they're being robbed by the enemy? It might be a place of moral failure, a place of deception, or a place where they simply lack wisdom. It's hard to bring those kinds of things to people's attention—there's always the danger that pride will get in the way, either yours or theirs!

Still, more vital than your emotional equilibrium is the call to serve one another in humility. And humility sometimes means taking the risk to point out your friend's enemy and then join him or her in battling that enemy. This is how you use truth and discernment to nourish and protect those you love, and how you receive the same service from them.

God, let my love for others exceed my habits of self-protection. And give me the humility to both approach others and be approachable.

day
244

Whoever wants to be great must become a servant. Whoever wants to be first among you must be your slave. That is what the Son of Man has done: He came to serve, not be served—and then to give away his life in exchange for the many who are held hostage.
Matthew 20:26–28 MSG

Forerunner

A forerunner is someone who comes before you and sets an example for you to follow. Someone who shows you how it's done.

Jesus was your forerunner in many ways, and serving was His forte. Jesus could have come as a mighty conquering hero, as the Jews expected. Or He could have come as an eloquent, wealthy politician. A power broker. Instead He came as a poor, uneducated woodworker from the "wrong side of the tracks." He came and gave everything He had, pouring out His love, laughter, life, and lessons to show people the beauty of the Rebellion.

Following the forerunner will take you to a place most people avoid—it takes you down in the eyes of the world. But from that low place of serving, you begin to tap the high purposes of God Himself.

God, let my life be a mirror of Yours, using all that I am to serve those You love in this world. Mentor me in ministry.

Be imitators of God, therefore, as dearly loved children and live a life of love, just as Christ loved us and gave himself up for us as a fragrant offering and sacrifice to God.
Ephesians 5:1–2 NIV

day 245

Imitate That Serve!

People usually imitate those they admire. Young children play out the roles of their parents with surprising accuracy. Teenagers model the dress, language, and values of popular culture. Young professionals absorb their corporate climate and subconsciously imitate their leaders. But Paul says plainly that the most profound example to pursue is that of God and His passionate love for planet Earth!

Imitate the compassion of Jesus. Imitate His attention to the unpopular people. Imitate His courage to confront falsehood. Imitate His willingness to sacrifice personal comfort for the chance to draw others into the New Rebellion. Imitate His prayer life. Imitate His discernment and passion for truth. Imitate His faith for miracles. Imitate His complete reliance upon the Father.

Don't stop there! Imitate His joy in the middle of hardships. Imitate His intimacy with His friends. Imitate His kindness and empathy.

Yes, God, this is the deep cry of my heart—to serve as You serve, to love as You love, and to obey You in all things.

day 246

He believed in the LORD; and He reckoned it to him as righteousness.
Genesis 15:6 NASB

The Road Less Traveled

Abraham is an amazing figure. With no Scriptures, with little known family history with God, he encountered God in a very personal way. The word of God came to him to leave everything known and secure and pursue a lofty but vague promise in an unknown land. And at the age of seventy-five, Abraham obeyed.

So how did an elderly pagan become the father of faith? Through one simple understanding—that he was not self-sufficient. Abraham grasped a core revelation that he needed something or someone outside himself to bring him into right relationship with God. And as God gave him a series of promises and commands over the next twenty-five years, Abraham trusted and obeyed, gambling his future upon this heavenly voice.

That trust invited the gift of righteousness and worked itself out in a life of holiness.

Help me, God, to trust You like Abraham, to follow Your direction even when I don't know where we're going. I choose a holy life.

From now on, think of it this way: Sin speaks a dead language that means nothing to you; God speaks your mother tongue, and you hang on every word. You are dead to sin and alive to God. That's what Jesus did.
Romans 6:11 MSG

day
247

Dead and Buried

Holiness is nothing you can work up through your own sweat. Holiness hinges upon one thing—whether sin has been fully addressed and dealt with in your life. Born into this world, you were born into sin. And although you had great desire for good things, when sin talked, you had to listen. Sin was in charge.

But God took care of that problem by killing you. By what?! By allowing you to share in the death of Christ that broke the tyranny of sin once and for all. Yep, your old sinful nature is dead and buried, and now you are ready to really live. To live in holiness, which means that you are empowered by God's Spirit to live the life you were created for! You hear the language God speaks and have the power to do what He says.

Thank You, precious God, for setting this captive heart free to live 100 percent for You. Let my life now be a holy life.

day
248

No matter which way I turn, I can't make myself do right. I want to, but I can't.
Romans 7:18 NLT

Acknowledging the Tension

So now sin no longer has mastery of your soul. You can finally hear and heed the voice of God. Hallelujah! But does that mean there is no more struggle against sin? Well, not quite.

This world is still marked by the presence of sin, and our souls still bear the mark of sin's influence, which means that you still feel pulled at times toward distrusting and disobeying the good heart of God. And until you enter the fullness of heaven, you will feel that tension.

This tension showcases your ongoing dependence upon the Spirit of God. Even though you are no longer a slave to sin, God calls you to embrace a lifelong submission to His empowering lordship in your life. Your holiness will always be the result of grace and not human effort!

God, I won't get frustrated in the struggle against sin; instead, I embrace Your strength, which demolishes sin and leads me into a holy life.

day 249

If your sinful nature controls your mind, there is death. But if the Holy Spirit controls your mind, there is life and peace.
Romans 8:6 NLT

A Good Fight = One You Win!

So there is a fight going on frequently in the hearts of God's people—a struggle between death and life. You have a choice over who will be in control—you can give away your hard-won freedom and let your sinful nature reassert its power. But why relinquish your liberty? When you grant the Holy Spirit His rightful place, He kicks out that old impostor of sin and leads you into the love, peace, and joy that characterize heaven.

Someone has said that a good fight is one you win. And Paul seems to agree. Twice he encouraged his student Timothy to "fight the good fight," and later acknowledged that he himself had "fought the good fight . . . finished the race . . . kept the faith" (1 Timothy 6:12; 2 Timothy 4:7 NKJV). When you fight alongside the Spirit of God, you're set to win.

Strengthen this heart, O God, so that I can fight against the insurgency of sin and maintain a Spirit-controlled life this day.

day 250

You were taught, with regard to your former way of life, to put off your old self, which is being corrupted by its deceitful desires; to be made new in the attitude of your minds; and to put on the new self, created to be like God in true righteousness and holiness.
Ephesians 4:22–24 NIV

The Real You

Have you figured out that there's a "real you" and an impostor? Your true self was "created to be like God"—isn't that extraordinary? Every child bears the image of the parent, and so your soul bears the divine imprint. You are designed for holiness!

So once your life comes under the rule of Jesus, holiness is now possible. Not perfection, mind you, but a very genuine life of alignment with the New Rebellion. Now that all the resources of God's Kingdom are behind you, your job is to partner with God in "putting off" and "putting on."

You have to consistently reaffirm your true identity by leaving behind old patterns of brokenness (the impostor) and stepping into God-patterns of new behavior. This is called holiness, and this is your inheritance from God. Enjoy it!

Keep me aligned today, God, with who I really am in You. Keep me from getting confused and reverting to that old impostor self.

day 251

*I*f anyone builds on the foundation with gold, silver, costly stones, wood, hay, or straw, each one's work will become obvious, for the day will disclose it.
1 Corinthians 3:12–13 HCSB

A Holy Fire

There is a lot that remains hidden in this world. It's hard enough to know your own heart and your own motivations, but when it comes to others, it's practically impossible. God promises that one day all that has been hidden will be revealed. At this time, people's true allegiances and activities will become known.

The first thing to be revealed will be the unparalleled majesty of God. The second thing will be an issue of righteousness—who will be covered by the righteousness of Jesus. The third thing will be an issue of holiness—what motivations, attitudes, words, and deeds have eternal value and which are worthless. Paul says they will be tested with fire: the worthless will be gone in a flash, but that which comes from a pure heart, empowered by the Spirit, will remain forever!

Test my heart now, God, and purify the motivations and expressions of my life so that they will last forever in Your Kingdom.

day
252

God . . . is the Lord of heaven and earth and . . . is not served by human hands, as if he needed anything, because he himself gives all men life and breath and everything else . . . God did this so that men would seek him and perhaps reach out for him and find him, though he is not far from each one of us.
Acts 17:24–25, 27 NIV

Unattainable yet Intimate

This passage attempts to capture in words part of the mystery of God's nature and purpose. He is completely above and beyond this world in the quality of His character—a character so different from yours that it requires a distinct word to describe it: *holiness*. Yet, despite the vast gulf of separation, He has come near! Very, very near, in fact.

God confounds our imagination by the unprecedented act of entering humanity and expressing His holiness in human terms. The vulnerability is astounding. The invitation to intimacy electrifying. Access to such a holiness arouses both our deepest longing and our strongest reticence. Yet He bridges the gap, embraces you in your uncertainty, and leads you into a life of holiness that mirrors His. His power becomes your strength, His love your confidence, His mission your own.

God, indeed You have not been far from me! By Your grace,
I have found You and been found by You.
Draw me into Your holiness.

I too am a man under authority, having soldiers under my command. I say to this one, "Go!" and he goes; and to another, "Come!" and he comes; and to my slave, "Do this!" and he does it.
Matthew 8:9 HCSB

day
253

The Basics

Authority flows out of the nature of God. His nature shapes His authority, and so it is with everyone—your nature defines your intrinsic authority. On top of that, people receive delegated authority through government, business, or other relationships. Whatever the level of authority that a person receives, there is a proportional amount of honor attached to it. Honor is the right response to authority, with both God and people.

Honor and authority are part of a right understanding of the New Rebellion, so when Jesus discovered an unusual grasp of this truth—in a Roman soldier, no less—He gave the man great praise. He hoped His disciples would get the same revelation—that they could trust the authority of God in their lives and also channel that authority out to others. This is the birthplace of faith and obedience.

God, open my understanding of this so I can both honor Your authority in my life and receive the authority You've given me.

day 254

Honor your father and your mother, as the LORD your God has commanded you, that your days may be prolonged and that it may go well with you on the land which the LORD your God gives you.
Deuteronomy 5:16 NASB

It Starts at Home

As the first authority every person experiences, parents are due great honor. And when honor is given, both the one giving and the one receiving honor are elevated. In fact, God promises a great blessing—many years and good years—for those who give this caliber of respect and appreciation to the authority of their parents.

Your parents may have been wise, loving parents, or they may have been quite the opposite, and their choices have had a huge impact on you. Still, their authority is real and so it falls to every young man and woman to honor everything that is worthy of honor. And where they are not worthy, you honor the position of their authority even when you can't honor the actions. Those who learn this Kingdom lesson will experience great blessings as a result!

God, no matter my age, I choose to love and honor those You gave me as parents. May we all experience Your blessing as a result.

Out of respect for Christ, be courteously reverent to one another. Wives, understand and support your husbands . . . Husbands, go all out in your love for your wives.
Ephesians 5:21–22, 25 MSG

day 255

And Continues in the Home

As you leave your family of origin and establish your own family, honor remains at the core of the home. Mutual honor between a wife and a husband is the essential ingredient for a happy and holy home life!

"Courteously reverent" is the way this translation puts it, which reflects the truth that every human bears the image of God and is due that measure of honor. Within the covenant of marriage, the commitment to honor is elevated even higher as that person is given an unparalleled position within your life. Only your commitment to God Himself exceeds it.

Divorce is the greatest dishonor that a marriage can experience, which is why God hates it so intensely. His call is to love those who have been injured by it and at the same time, set a new standard of honor within the New Rebellion.

God, let my honor for You be expressed powerfully this day toward my spouse, or the one who may become my spouse.

day 256

The elders who direct the affairs of the church well are worthy of double honor, especially those whose work is preaching and teaching.
1 Timothy 5:17 NIV

Your Spiritual Leaders

If honor is a big deal to God, then "double honor" must be significant indeed. And it is. But why would your church leaders be worthy of double honor? Well, first they are due honor as a child of God and part of your spiritual community. But their leadership gift has resulted in their receiving additional authority within the community, and additional honor is the godly response to that.

This isn't to improperly elevate a person and make them a celebrity; "celebrity worship" is not real honor for it denies the delegated quality of authority. But within the New Rebellion, God's people give extra respect and appreciation to those who bear the weight of leadership among the church, especially those who study and impart God's truths to others. This is part of how you honor God as the Giver of those leadership gifts.

God, show me how to intentionally honor and bless those whom You have placed in my life as spiritual leaders.

day 257

Show respect for everyone. Love your Christian
brothers and sisters. Fear God.
Show respect for the king.
1 Peter 2:17 NLT

A Prevailing Attitude

You honor yourself when you honor others appropriately. Likewise, if you are disrespectful to people in general and to leaders in particular, you highlight your own lack of honor and self-respect.

When you live the New Rebellion, you are gripped by a desire to love God, love others, and love yourself (see Mark 12:30–31). This attitude of love breeds a natural flow of honor to everyone in your world, according to their intrinsic worth as well as their place of authority. Every person deserves a certain amount of respect and honor, as Peter declares here, no matter how "low" their station in life. Your brothers and sisters in Christ deserve additional honor. Of course, God deserves the highest honor of all. And those with governmental authority deserve a unique honor—even if they are in the "wrong" political party!

God, increase my love for all those You have placed in my world so that I will honor them in a way that honors You.

day 258

He who scorns instruction will pay for it, but he who respects a command is rewarded.
Proverbs 13:13 NIV

Consequences

Assuming that the instruction or command you receive is coming from someone who has legitimate authority in your life, it is vital that you respect this kind of direction. When you do, you build favor and when you don't, you undermine yourself and your future. The reward or the penalty you earn is not merely a natural one; God pays attention to the flow of honor or dishonor that comes from your life, and there are spiritual rewards and penalties that amplify the natural ones.

It gets tricky when the authority in your life is less than wise or just. But even here, when you obey the direction that comes, as long as it isn't unethical, you earn favor and blessing because you are responding correctly to God-given authority. This is important in the New Rebellion.

God, I want to lead a life that is favored by
You and others. Help me to initiate that
life through honoring others well.

day 259

There is no authority except from God, and those that exist are instituted by God. So then, the one who resists the authority is opposing God's command, and those who oppose it will bring judgment on themselves.
Romans 13:1–2 HCSB

The Bottom Line

Here Paul finally lays it all out on the table. Authority is God's idea and reflects an eternal value from heaven. This means that your parent, your teacher, your boss, your elected official—they are all there because God intends you to have authority figures in your life. So even if one of those authorities disrespects the authority of God—or disrespects you!—you can honor God by respecting and honoring them. When you do, you represent the Kingdom of God to them, whether or not they appreciate it.

On the other hand, if you resist their authority by disrespecting them, talking bad about them to others, or disobeying their direction, you are essentially resisting God Himself, and you don't want to be doing that! Favor is your goal, not judgment. And eventually you will find favor as the reward of honor.

Mold my perspective, God, so I can see the authorities in my life as expressions of Yourself and give them the honor they deserve.

day 260

Watch your life and doctrine closely. Persevere in them, because if you do, you will save both yourself and your hearers.
1 Timothy 4:16 NIV

Quitters Never Win

Doctrine is a fancy word for how you see God. What makes up your understanding and view of Him? Do you see Him as a fierce old man who is disappointed with you? Is He unapproachable, judgmental, and legalistic? Only loving those who fast and pray enough? Or is He the kindest person you've ever met, using His power and wisdom for your blessing and prosperity? Your view of God will determine the life you lead and your impact upon the world.

Because your relationship with God is so pivotal, it requires diligent protection. A lot of things will attack it—difficulty, disappointment, and distraction, among them. And this is where perseverance is required. To go the distance. To safeguard the core of your identity and conviction. To advance the Rebellion. You can't afford to give up or get pulled off course.

God, I trust You to guard my life and protect my view of You. With Your help, I won't give up or get distracted from what really matters.

day 261

God blesses the people who patiently endure testing. Afterward they will receive the crown of life that God has promised to those who love him.
James 1:12 NLT

Patience Gets the Reward

Not many in America know what it's like to be persecuted for their faith, but there are other ways that your faith gets tested, aren't there. The loss of a job. The loss of a loved one. The loss of a dream. There are many ways that your confidence in God's goodness might be shaken.

When you suffer, there is a human part that turns to God and says, "Why?" But it's right at this vulnerable place where God wants to reveal Himself to you and restore your confidence in Him. Those who trust in the face of testing find a fellowship with God that empowers them to live out the New Rebellion in greater dimension. Not only will you be enlarged through the process, you will also receive the reward of greater intimacy and authority with God.

God, suffering is hard. Help me to find You right in the middle of it and become the Rebel You want me to be.

day 262

Do you see what this means—all these pioneers who blazed the way, all these veterans cheering us on? It means we'd better get on with it. Strip down, start running—and never quit!
Hebrews 12:1 MSG

Peer Pressure

Peer pressure usually has a negative connotation—the pressure to compromise your convictions, for instance. But peer pressure can also be good. It can be the expectation of others that you will never quit your pursuit of God and His Kingdom.

Picture yourself walking down a long hallway in an old castle. On each side of the hall are pictures whose faces look out at you. These are the men and women who have gone before you and secured their reward in heaven. Hear them speak to you now: "Go, go, go! You are doing great; you have what it takes. Don't look back and don't quit. The pain of the race is worth it all!"

This is real! They really do cheer you on, calling you to live your best life and serve the Rebellion with perseverance.

God, I devote my life to Your cause—I will never give up.
I accept the peer pressure, the encouragement of all
who have gone before me.

Take up the full armor of God, so that you will be able to resist in the evil day, and having done everything, to stand firm.
Ephesians 6:13 NASB

day 263

Stand

In most battles, the one who wins is the last one standing. The same is true in your daily battle of faith. In many cases, it's not great knowledge or skill that preserves you but rather perseverance. You just won't stop loving God and loving others, no matter what!

To empower you to stand firm, God has given you spiritual armor and weaponry that are more powerful than any tool of the enemy. Your equipment is character—God's character and yours. Those who know who God is, and know who they are as God's representatives, cannot be defeated. They resist evil, and find that the goodness of Christ overcomes it. They do the things they know to do—they pray, they believe, they obey, and they win. When God backs you up, the enemy will back down, and you'll be left standing.

Thank You, God, for giving me everything I need to stand up to my spiritual enemies, to persevere, and to win.

day 264

We must not get tired of doing good, for we will reap at the proper time if we don't give up.
Galatians 6:9 HCSB

Second Wind

One of the effects of sin in this world is weariness—in fact, God spoke this directly to Adam (see Genesis 3:17–19). Even when you are doing the right things and doing a good job of them, there are times when you just get tired of it. This is where the quality of perseverance shows itself—when you don't give up or let yourself get distracted by more-entertaining but less-profitable endeavors.

The New Rebellion isn't a big blaze of glory. It's a day-in, day-out commitment to what's important. It's an enduring focus upon God and His interests over the long haul. It's about prioritizing relationships over activities and intimacy with God above all. When this operates in your life, there is a tremendous harvest—incrementally through this life and the big blaze of glory at the end.

God, be the center of my attention throughout my days, keeping me focused and faithful upon the good things of Your choosing.

My dear brothers, stand firm. Let nothing move you. Always give yourselves fully to the work of the Lord, because you know that your labor in the Lord is not in vain.
1 Corinthians 15:58 NIV

day
265

Don't Get Distracted

Your spiritual enemy is a master of deception and discouragement. One of his chief lies is that all your efforts for God are worthless, and there's nothing to show for it. This is a lie.

A Kingdom perspective is a long-range perspective. When you plant a garden, you can't become disheartened because the plants aren't grown the next day. There's a lot of waiting in gardening, and there's a lot of waiting in life. The effects of your decisions are often not seen until weeks or months or years later. And in this sense, every labor in the soil is an act of faith that the reward will come.

So Paul exhorts you once again: "Stand firm." Don't be discouraged or distracted. Stay focused on Kingdom issues with Kingdom perspective. Eventually, maybe sooner than you think, you will see Kingdom results!

God, I know that the One who makes the plants grow will be faithful to finish what You've started in my life.

day 266

Keep your eyes open, hold tight to your convictions, give it all you've got, be resolute, and love without stopping.
1 Corinthians 16:13–14 MSG

Resolutions

At the beginning of each new year it's popular to make "resolutions" for the coming year. But resolutions are more than wishes or even promises—they are things you are "resolute" about, activities you are fully committed to. What captures your heart with that kind of passion?

When the founding fathers penned the Declaration of Independence, they wrote, "Resolved that . . ." These were not passing fancies, no mere inspiration of the moment; these were principles and actions to which they pledged their lives, knowing that they may well pay for them with their lives.

The New Rebellion requires that same level of conviction and commitment. If you want to change the world, and be changed in the process, your dedication to serve others in the love of God must be unwavering. You must be resolute.

Yes, God, I am resolved! With Your strength, I will be focused and passionate, holding my convictions tightly, giving it all I've got.

My dear lover glows with health—red-blooded, radiant! . . . His words are kisses, his kisses words.
Everything about him delights me,
thrills me through and through!
Song of Songs 5:10, 16 MSG

day 267

God Is a Lover!

This unusual book of the Bible is a love story between King Solomon and a Shunammite woman. Many have wondered just why it was included in the Scriptures, but the best answer is that it gives an entirely fresh perspective on your love affair with God. He is the pursuer of your heart, and every romantic desire you possess is the reflection of His great passion for you.

The thrill and wonder of romantic love are qualities that wise couples sustain over decades of intimacy. And in such a way, the radiance and fascination of your heavenly romance can consume your thoughts and actions for a lifetime. Just as you can never reach the end of knowing your spouse, the infinite character of God is a source of unceasing discovery and delight. Don't settle for less!

Enlarge my passion for You, dear God. Let my words be kisses to Your soul and Your words kisses to mine.

day 268

Do nothing out of rivalry or conceit, but in humility consider others as more important than yourselves.
Philippians 2:3 HCSB

Elevation

The key to good romance is a radical purity of love. And the core of love is living for another's good, not your own. Much of what passes for romance in the world is mutual self-seeking. But that caliber of "love" won't get you very far—pretty soon, selfishness reveals itself and alienates the other person.

But God, the Author of romance, spelled it out in the Scriptures: Elevate others. Don't seek your own gain, but look for ways to honor and uplift other people! And not only did He spell it out, He lived it out in the life of Jesus. He showed the world what humility looks like. There was no rivalry or conceit in anything He did; instead, He elevated everyone who would receive His priceless love. This is the model for the New Rebellion.

Help me to be a giver, God, not a taker. Let the romance in my life exhibit my elevation of others. Beginning today.

Flee from sexual immorality. All other sins a man commits are outside his body, but he who sins sexually sins against his own body.
1 Corinthians 6:18 NIV

day 269

Romance Gone Bad

Sex outside marriage is a temptation and pitfall to many. At first glance, it doesn't appear to hurt anybody, so what's the big deal? Yet it does hurt somebody—actually, it hurts everybody! Why? Because it is motivated by selfishness, by the desire to take something that doesn't belong to you.

What does it mean to sin against your own body? For starters, there are the very real dangers of sexually transmitted diseases. Next, sexual sin robs your current or future spouse—you can no longer give them your best. Beyond that, immorality robs your very soul because in the intimacy of this union, you give part of yourself to that person. Within marriage, this strengthens your oneness; outside marriage, it fragments and steals.

God's grace redeems and restores, but God's Rebels boldly lift up the standard of purity.

God, grant me the wisdom and conviction to keep myself 100 percent pure in mind and body so I can bring my best to my marriage.

day 270

A man shall leave his father and his mother, and be joined to his wife; and they shall become one flesh.
Genesis 2:24 NASB

Romance Gone Right

This is the mind-boggling potential of a woman and a man in marriage—to become "one flesh." To enter into a level of lifelong partnership that has never been experienced before and will never exist in any other dimension. A true union of passion and purpose that brings two very distinct souls into a shared existence and allows each to receive the gifts and destiny of the other.

However, this promise of merging can take place only within the boundaries God describes: when the husband sets aside all other emotional attachments and priorities in order to give his full allegiance to his new wife. And the wife does the same. This union must be untouchable, a sacred space. When this occurs, a whole new destiny in the New Rebellion is fashioned for them, a calling they can fulfill only in complete togetherness.

God, thank You for such a wondrous hope. I will never set my sights lower than this high calling to romantic partnership.

Husbands, go all out in your love for your wives, exactly as Christ did for the church—a love marked by giving, not getting. Christ's love makes the church whole. His words evoke her beauty. Everything he does and says is designed to bring the best out of her.
Ephesians 5:25–26 MSG

day 271

Bringing Out the Best

The glory of marriage—not only is it the pinnacle of human intimacy, it is the clearest window into the intimacy God desires to have with you! Wow.

This chapter in Ephesians parallels the self-sacrificing love between a man and his wife with the relationship between Christ and His church. Jesus' continuous giving of Himself for people is the standard of love to be found between a husband and a wife. Their heaven-birthed love for one another will always elevate the other, never withdraw or hide. Their loving service to each other will bring wholeness to places of brokenness. Their words will reach deep and draw out the latent beauty of the other!

Have the courage to reach for the best in your spouse! Take the risk to serve well. Real love recognizes and affirms the true value and calling of your partner.

Search me and know me, God. Wash away all that falls short of love, and let me channel Your unending love to the one I'm made for.

day 272

Two are better than one, because they have a good reward for their labor. For if they fall, one will lift up his companion. But woe to him who is alone when he falls, for he has no one to help him up . . . Though one may be overpowered by another, two can withstand him. Ecclesiastes 4:9–10, 12 NKJV

The Power of Two

King Solomon, who wrote these wise words, recognized the amazing synergy of partnership. He observed that, in companionship, one plus one equals *three*. Because of the opportunity to bring the best out in the one you love, not only are you joining the strengths and assets of one to those of another; you are activating new abilities that were only resident in potential. The relationship itself brings them to life. What a God-thing!

In the Garden of Eden, only one thing failed to receive God's endorsement as "good." "It is *not good*," He said, "for the man to be alone" (Genesis 2:18 NIV). Aloneness causes a person's potential to wither while community brings it to life! Within the oneness of marriage, two people are encouraged, challenged, equipped, and stretched. Neither will fall down and stay down; neither will be overpowered.

God, instill in me the character and commitment to be that kind of empowering partner for the one You join me to.

How good and pleasant it is when brothers live together in unity! It is like precious oil poured on the head, running down on the beard, running down on Aaron's beard, down upon the collar of his robes . . . For there the LORD bestows His blessing, even life forevermore.
Psalm 133:1–3 NIV

day 273

Better Together

Everyone has observed the tragedy of marriages that are not at all good or pleasant. Divorce is a ravishing plague upon our planet, and even those who remain married often live without the blessings of real unity. Unity does not come easily or cheaply—it requires a constant death to self. But isn't that self so much better off dead?

For those who make the investment of humility and reap the harvest of unity, the rewards are many. A life that is good and pleasant is a great beginning, but it doesn't stop there. This is the place of true blessing, both in the natural realm and the spiritual. And, it's the place of authority that can change your world! The reference to Aaron the high priest conveys the spiritual authority that will arise within your holy partnership.

God, lead me into this quality of character that invests itself in humility and unity in all my relationships, especially marriage.

day 274

"Bring the whole tithe into the storehouse, that there may be food in my house. Test me in this," says the LORD Almighty, "and see if I will not throw open the floodgates of heaven and pour out so much blessing that you will not have room enough for it."
Malachi 3:10 NIV

The Reward of Obedience

Do you believe that God can supply every need you have? But do you believe that He *will* supply? Can you imagine that your heavenly Father would bless your life so much that you wouldn't even know what to do with it all? This is His promise to you, an essential principle that God desires to release through you into the world.

The practice of tithing—giving 10 percent of your earnings back to God—is a powerful statement into the spiritual realm that all 100 percent of your finances belongs to the New Rebellion. But far from being stingy, God is looking for ways to release His blessings upon the earth—and so He issues you a challenge. Test Him through the obedience of tithing and see if God won't reward you lavishly, in ways both natural and spiritual.

Generous God, my Giver, I honor You with all I have because I know everything comes from You. Bless me so I can be a blessing to others.

Then Elijah said to her, "Do not fear; go, do as you have said, but make me a little bread cake from it first and bring it out to me, and afterward you may make one for yourself and for your son."
1 Kings 17:13 NASB

day
275

The Reward of Generosity

Have you observed miracles? Miracles are the stuff of God's Kingdom and they still happen today, every day. In fact, God wants to do miracles through you!

Elijah was a man who moved in God's power all the time. But this was a hard time in Israel—a drought had ravaged the land and the hearts of many. When Elijah asked this woman for a meal, she complained that she was already preparing her last one. In the face of looming tragedy, Elijah asked the woman for a step of faith—an act of trust and kindness in the midst of her bitterness. And she responded.

As a result, this Rebel opened her heart to encounter the goodness of God in a very practical way. For the remainder of the drought, her jars of oil and flour were miraculously filled each day.

Help me, God, to not be afraid when my needs are great but to look to You as the miraculous God who provides.

day 276

No one can be a slave of two masters, since either he will hate one and love the other, or be devoted to one and despise the other. You cannot be slaves of God and of money.
Matthew 6:24 HCSB

Only Room for One on the Throne

Jesus was really getting "in your face" with this description of money and the human heart. Can you feel the power of His challenge? Who will ultimately be Lord of your life? Money can be a powerful force for good, but it has the ability like little else to grab the throne in your life. As it has so many.

Jesus spoke often about money to His disciples, urging them toward the freedom of using money, but not being used by it. Those enslaved by money find their attention and devotion captivated by it, their thoughts and actions manipulated by its influence. Even worse, the control of money is inherently antagonistic toward the rightful call of Christ. In the face of this, Jesus is direct: Rebel against that false tyrant and choose the freedom of being a slave to God!

Spirit, lead me and be in control of my motives, thoughts, and intentions. Your way is the best and leads to joy.

God, I embrace You as my Master and desire Your rule above all else in my life. Don't allow my loyalties to be compromised by money.

day 277

The borrower is servant to the lender.
Proverbs 22:7 NLT

Who Is Serving Whom?

Money is a practical resource for living. It releases energy to accomplish things that you value—whether your values include paying for a house or a vacation or a big-screen TV. But more than that, money is meant to be a resource of the Kingdom of God. The potential of money is to reflect His values and interests in the earth. That's the goal.

One of the pitfalls that can hinder this Kingdom goal is debt. Not that debt is inherently bad, but it does bring a very real servitude along with it, as King Solomon noted. And because of that, debt should be entered very cautiously . . . so that money can serve you and serve God's purposes and not the other way around! God's Rebels play by the rules of heaven, not the rules of earth.

Help me to be wise, God, and avoid unnecessary entanglements with debt. Let every resource of mine be a resource of Yours!

day 278

I have been young, and now am old; yet I have not seen the righteous forsaken, nor his descendants begging bread. He is ever merciful, and lends; and his descendants are blessed.
Psalm 37:25–26 NKJV

God, the Great Resourcer

King David had been around the block a few times and seen many things in his lifetime, but he had never seen someone following God who was out on the streets asking for handouts. This speaks loudly of God's commitment to you as His Rebel. He takes seriously your well-being . . . and not only yours, but those who will come after you.

There is a small qualification: God's Rebels must be "righteous" Rebels. It is your responsibility to be in fellowship with God. To be listening to and obeying His voice. When you invest yourself in the purposes of God, you will find yourself resourced by the infinite provision of God. Then you can rest in the truth that you cannot be forgotten by the One who knows you by name. He is fully invested in you!

Thank You, God. I know You will never leave me. I know You will provide for me so that I can give generously to others.

day
279

Whoever loves money never has money enough; whoever loves wealth is never satisfied with his income. This too is meaningless.
Ecclesiastes 5:10 NIV

Grasping After the Wind

King Solomon knew about money. Just about everything that you could imagine having—he had it. Lots of money, jewels, mansions, the coolest transportation, beautiful people to serve him, power, and an extraordinary wisdom! But Solomon struggled with it and spent many years experimenting to see what passions really satisfied.

Eventually he realized that possessions tend to create an insatiable appetite for more possessions if they own your heart. So if money becomes the motivating force of your life, you are embarking upon a never-ending, never-satisfying journey. It is a meaningless pursuit, and many rich people could vouch for that reality.

The discovery of Solomon is that money is not worthy of your life's ambition. Only God is. God is obtainable, infinite, and satisfies the heart fully. This releases the transforming power of contentment. Right alignment with value will change the world.

God, by Your help I will love people and use things, not vice versa. Only You can really satisfy and keep my heart free.

day 280

My choice is you, GOD, first and only. And now I find I'm your choice! You set me up with a house and yard. And then you made me your heir!
Psalm 16:5–6 MSG

Destined for Goodness

God loves you just the way you are and not as you should be. Experience the love of a God who declares that you are His first choice. You! *You* are destined for greatness and for goodness. He chose you from the beginning of the world and has given you the wealth that belongs to His children. Talk about an inheritance!

In this psalm David revels in the generosity of God that provides both the needs of his circumstances and the longings of his heart. He caught a glimpse of the bigness of God and realized he need never worry again. There is no difficulty or lack that God cannot supply in lavish measure. As a man or woman of the Kingdom, your life is a demonstration, not of unlimited money, but of unlimited provision from God! You are an heir.

God, show me what it means to be Your heir, to own a heavenly inheritance upon the earth. You are my full supply.

Do you not know that your body is a temple of the Holy Spirit, who is in you, whom you have received from God? You are not your own; you were bought at a price. Therefore honor God with your body.

1 Corinthians 6:19–20 NIV

day 281

Body by God

The physical body is subject to two extremes—to neglect and to idolatry. The solution to both these sins lies in recognizing that your body, fashioned in the image of God, is meant to reflect the glory of God. After all, it's not about you; it's all about God! So honor Him with all you possess, including your physical health and appearance.

It's simple, really. Good health honors your body and honors God, the Maker of your body. Bad health dishonors Him. Being greatly overweight or underweight dishonors Him. The clothes you wear, the style of your hair, your makeup, your hygiene—all these things draw attention either to God or to yourself. But as a Kingdom Rebel, your passion is for Him! As the designer of your body, He alone deserves the honor you reflect.

Thank You, God, for the gift of my body. Let me honor it and consistently use it to showcase Your glory in my world.

day 282

Well, it may be true that the body is only a temporary thing, but that's no excuse for stuffing your body with food, or indulging it with sex. Since the Master honors you with a body, honor him with your body!
1 Corinthians 6:13 MSG

Garbage In, Garbage Out

Most of the Bible's direction on health comes in the form of correcting neglect. In essence, do *not* abuse your body! It is a holy thing. Do not abuse it with food—either too much, too little, or the wrong kinds. That means if you load up on food that is processed, packaged, and sweet, you're being foolish. Emphasize the food God Himself created—natural and fresh. And don't abuse your body with substances you know are harmful.

Sex, like food, is a gift from God and meant to be a source of extraordinary delight. But God knows, and explains, how to enjoy it to the maximum: with one person for a lifetime. And you can't improve on God's design. When you abuse God's pleasures, you damage your body and fail to reflect His glory in the world.

God, grant me the spiritual fruit of self-control
so that both my diet and my sexuality
bring great honor to Your name.

day
283

I discipline my body like an athlete,
training it to do what it should.
1 Corinthians 9:27 NLT

Ready for Anything

So was Paul an Iron Man triathlete? Probably not. Yet Paul knew that his physical body was entrusted with a monumental task—that of proclaiming the gospel and planting churches around the Mediterranean. Not only was God's honor at stake in his body, but Paul's mission depended upon his ongoing health and vitality.

Like Paul, you do not have the authority to abuse or neglect your body. This is God's property. Which means a sedentary lifestyle that hurts the body is a sin. You may or may not know what God will require of your life, but a healthy body and full span of years will no doubt be necessary to fulfill that calling. Paul took this very seriously, and so should you. Exercise your body. Be strong and fit—not for the attention of others but for the needs of the Rebellion.

God, I want to be ready for anything and everything
You call me to do. I don't ever want my
obedience hindered by my health.

day 284

It is vain for you to rise up early, to sit up late,
to eat the bread of sorrows; for so He
gives His beloved sleep.
Psalm 127:2 NKJV

Don't Toss This Gift

Another way in which God's Rebels steward their health is by guarding their physical energy. Sleep is a true gift from God, one to be received with respect and gratitude. When money and production become the taskmaster, people are driven to work relentlessly without adequate time for rest and renewal. This is foolish and counterproductive. More important, it is disobedient to God and robs your effectiveness in the Kingdom.

It is a holy thing to embrace the work God has called you to. And then it is a holy thing to stop and rest—a pattern modeled by God Himself. This pattern acknowledges our dependency upon God as well as His sufficiency for the task. The Sabbath-lifestyle was important enough to be included in the Ten Commandments, and it is meant to be lived out in your work and sleep each day.

Forgive me, God, for the times I have dishonored
my body by robbing its rest. I gratefully
receive Your generous gift of sleep.

Do not be wise in your own eyes; fear the LORD and turn away from evil. It will be healing to your body and refreshment to your bones.
Proverbs 3:7–8 NASB

Make Your Body Happy

Many medical doctors today acknowledge that long-term anger can weaken the body's defenses and make the body more receptive to infection and the creation of a stomach ulcer, and that other unresolved emotional issues have seriously damaging effects upon the body. This dynamic reflects God's intentional connection between the spiritual and natural dimensions of the earth. Physical things matter to God—and they often communicate hidden realities.

Not only does God call you to build and maintain a healthy body, He also says that your spiritual condition will affect your physical health, for good or bad (see Proverbs 14:30; 17:22). This is good news! This means that earnest pursuit of God will have good effects upon your body. Something like spiritual vitamins. Cool.

Let's summarize: Your plan for a healthy body will include a nutritious diet, a well-directed sexuality, a wholesome appearance, regular exercise, adequate sleep, *and* a vital spiritual life!

Lead me to a healthy life, inside and out, God.
Not by following legalistic rules but by receiving
Your wisdom into my heart.

day 286

At the end of the ten days they looked healthier and
better nourished than any of the young men
who ate the royal food.
Daniel 1:15 NIV

Physical Favor

Daniel was a bold player in the Rebellion. Although he was a prisoner of war, he and other Hebrew royalty were being integrated into the Babylonian royalty. But this gave rise to some points of conflict. To obey God while honoring their new government was a fine line, and God gave Daniel the wisdom to walk it with excellence.

When required to eat food that would defile their consciences, they proposed a healthy alternative—a diet of vegetables and water in place of the king's delicacies. The catch was that their strength and appearance must not suffer. The result of this ten-day experiment was that Daniel and his friends exceeded all the others who were in the same training program. And true to form, their physical health played an important role in the adventures God eventually led them into.

Make me a Daniel in my day, God. Give me the courage and commitment to build a strong spirit and a strong body for Your sake.

day 287

Who has known the Lord's mind, that he may instruct Him? But we have the mind of Christ.
1 Corinthians 2:16 HCSB

Go Mental

Another aspect of honoring God in your body is cultivating an active and educated mind. The ability to reason, discern, and decide is another immense gift from God and reflects God's own capabilities. It's part of the divine image you bear.

This brings two tasks to bear upon those in the New Rebellion—first, the development of your natural mental abilities. It is to the honor of God and the activation of your destiny that you read, study, and learn many things about the physical and spiritual worlds God created. The Scriptures are an infinite storehouse. People of wisdom are another resource.

On top of that, you are tasked with the development of a spiritual gift: the mind of Christ. When you cultivate your spiritual sensitivity, you'll learn to hear God's Spirit within you, leading you with the wisdom of heaven.

Shape my mind, God, and let me think Your thoughts. Cause me to understand what's important and grow in wisdom this day.

day 288

The weapons of our warfare are not fleshly, but are powerful through God for the demolition of strongholds.
2 Corinthians 10:4 HCSB

Slap Down

You are at war.

No one came into this world wanting to be at war; nevertheless, spiritual war is a reality. There is an enemy who seeks to diminish the glory of your life and ultimately the glory of God. But there is some good news. The good news is that you are on the winning side!

What is crucial to understand is that you're not at war with people or politicians or other religions; your enemy is a spiritual enemy. Fortunately, so are your weapons spiritual. The millions of men and women who compose the New Rebellion are God's representatives in the world, bearing His authority, and moving in His power. He has equipped you for battle, and your weapons are effective because He is God. His purposes in the world will be accomplished, and you're part of that.

Strengthen me, God, to war well in this Rebellion. Teach me the art of spiritual battle for Your glory and Your purposes.

day
289

Be sober, be vigilant; because your adversary the devil walks about like a roaring lion, seeking whom he may devour. Resist him.

1 Peter 5:8–9 NKJV

Yes, Virginia, There Is a Devil

The New Rebellion implies that there is something to rebel *against*. Several things, actually: Satan, the world system, and your own flesh. All three of these resist the purposes of God and must be resisted in return.

Even as a child of God whose nature has been redeemed by Christ, you retain a source of inner misguidance the Bible calls "the flesh," which seeks its own will, not God's. In alliance with your flesh, the world system is a collection of motivations, attitudes, and social structures that reflect the goals of the Adversary, Satan.

Against this enemy, Peter challenges you to be smart, be aware. Don't be naive about his destructive intentions. His agenda must be resisted by you, and you have what it takes. Your true nature, directed by the Holy Spirit, is redeemed and powerful against every enemy.

Wake me up, God. Tune me in. Cause me to be vigilant to see the works of the Adversary and take a stand against them.

day 290

Be strong in the Lord and in the strength of His might. Put on the full armor of God, so that you will be able to stand firm against the schemes of the devil.
Ephesians 6:10–11 NASB

Geared Up

God has provided everything you need for victory in the spiritual arena. But it's not automatic. You're not a passive player in this cosmic drama; you're an empowered partner.

As a soldier of the Kingdom, *you* have to strengthen yourself in the Lord; *you* are the one who must find and assume your identity in Him. His armor will simply sit there until *you* put it on! Jesus has given you every spiritual resource and weapon. Your part is to understand the armor, pick it up, and move in it. When you do, you will be invincible. The devil cannot resist you when you are moving in the will and strength of God.

Your enemy does have schemes and strategies, but through experience you will discern them and foil them. What a privilege to participate in such eternal matters!

I'm ready to do my part, God, and partner
with heaven against the schemes of the devil.
Lead me and empower me today.

"Yes," he told them, "I saw Satan falling from heaven as a flash of lightning! And I have given you authority over all the power of the enemy, and you can walk among snakes and scorpions and crush them."
Luke 10:18–19 NLT

Authority!

Jesus had just commissioned seventy of His disciples to go out in pairs through the villages, doing what Jesus Himself did—sharing the good news and doing miracles. Make no mistake: this was an act of spiritual warfare! God's truth confronted the lies of the world system. Miracles were a power confrontation against the bondage of sin.

And it worked! Hundreds were saved, healed, and delivered. When they returned, Jesus broke into joyful commentary: His authority had been effectively multiplied through His disciples, and Satan's power had been shaken to its core. The handwriting was on the wall—Satan would not long resist the Rebellion because his authority was superseded.

Now it's your turn to bring down Satan through the authority of Christ. There is no spiritual enemy that can stand against you. You will crush them as He did!

Let my authority be multiplied this day, God.
I am Your disciple, and I bear Your
cause in joy and confidence.

day 292

The Messenger-Angel showed me the high priest Joshua. He was standing before GOD's angel where the Accuser showed up to accuse him. Then GOD said to the Accuser, "I, GOD, rebuke you, Accuser!" Zechariah 3:1–2 MSG

My Dad's Bigger Than Your Dad

One of your enemy's chief tactics is accusation. Do you know that voice? The one that says, "You didn't read your Bible today—what spiritual authority could you possibly have? You've been selfish and rude to your family; what kind of Christian *are* you? Besides, you've never done any *real* miracles. Give it up."

When God's people returned from Babylon to their homeland, they began to rebuild the Temple and the city of Jerusalem. But after the foundation was laid, their work was forcibly stopped for almost twenty years! The high priest Joshua was facing serious accusation from Satan: "You're a failure. This Temple's never going to happen. Give it up!" But through the encouragement of Zechariah, God shut up that paralyzing voice, and strengthened Joshua to fulfill his destiny. Joshua learned something that day about overcoming the Accuser in spiritual warfare.

Show me where I have listened to the Accuser, God.
I'm not going to give him the satisfaction of
diverting me from my mission.

day 293

"In your anger do not sin": Do not let the sun go down while you are still angry, and do not give the devil a foothold.
Ephesians 4:26–27 NIV

Battle Strategies

As any warrior in training, you have to learn the enemy's strategies and then learn counterstrategies to defeat them. Here's a powerful skill to brush up on: forgiveness.

The enemy's plan is to instigate some injustice against you so that you'll become angry against another person or situation. He knows that as soon as you allow anger to rule your heart, even if it remains hidden from anyone else, he will have a "foothold." He will have access to lure you into greater sin through guilt, bitterness, gossip, envy, etc.

But Paul uncovers his scheme and offers the solution. Before the sun goes down each day, examine your heart; if you find anger, deal with it immediately! In no case allow yourself to go to bed with unresolved anger in your heart. Wise up to the enemy's strategies and outsmart him.

I get it, God. This is one skill I'm going to learn and learn well. I pledge myself to be vigilant against anger and offense.

day 294

The thief comes only to steal and kill and destroy; I came that they may have life, and have it abundantly. John 10:10 NASB

Can't Touch This!

Could the battle lines be drawn any more clearly? Your enemy brings death where God brings life. And it's not just *life*, it's *abundant life*. It's life without limitation, absolutely overflowing beyond imagination. "Eternal life" it's often called, but you don't have to wait for heaven to get it. Eternal life is not only without boundaries in its length; it is without measure in its breadth. In other words, God intends to give you a quality of life that is immeasurable in its goodness!

You can always recognize the thief because he will instigate situations that try to take what belongs to you. He will tempt you to attitudes and actions that bring death inside. There may be an appealing appearance—thus, the temptation—but the product of the enemy's lies is always to rob you blind.

God, I'm asking You for the prudence to see ahead and recognize the results of different actions so that I can choose life every time.

day 295

"We are witnesses of everything [Jesus] did in the country of the Jews and in Jerusalem . . ." While Peter was still speaking these words, the Holy Spirit came on all who heard the message.
Acts 10:39, 44 NIV

The Power of Story

You have a story, a history of loss and love. In circumstances as unique as yourself, you experienced the person of Jesus, just as Peter did. Your story of redemption is your own, and no one can take it from you. And although you are more than your story, it has fashioned you in many important ways. It will always be part of the message of your life.

When Peter was led by a miraculous vision to the home of Cornelius, he was compelled to share both the truth *and* his experience with the truth. It wasn't just Jesus' words that had changed Peter's life; it was the person of Christ. It was walking with Him and experiencing His life over the course of several years. Now, when you tell your story, you can expect the Holy Spirit to show up!

Empower my story, God, so that it can become a part of other people's stories and lead them to their own encounter with You.

day
296

Peter and John answered and said to them, "Whether it is right in the sight of God to listen to you more than to God, you judge. For we cannot but speak the things which we have seen and heard."
Acts 4:19–20 NKJV

Marked for Life

Peter, now joined by John, was forced to defend his preaching and healing before the Jewish priests in Jerusalem. The council feared this new movement would threaten their power in the community and so they warned Peter and John to stop teaching about Jesus. But these courageous men had a story to tell, and they would not be silenced by such intimidation.

The things they had "seen and heard" through the ministry of Jesus had changed them forever—as you have been changed! And now you, too, speak of what He has done in your life. The life of Christ compels you to share your story and to serve the New Rebellion. No one can challenge your experience with God. It stands on its own and releases the power of the gospel to those who hear it.

Release my tongue to tell my story, God. Whether it comes to one or hundreds, let it flow with the same power as the stories of these mighty men.

An angel of the Lord spoke to Philip saying, "Get up and go south to the road that descends from Jerusalem to Gaza." . . . So he got up and went; and there was an Ethiopian.
Acts 8:26–27 NASB

day 297

Divine Appointments

God has a way of planning divine appointments. He sends people into your path—maybe even today!—and opens the opportunity for conversation and connection. Sometimes it's just a moment, and sometimes it's lengthy, but either way it's a breath of heaven upon the earth. Learn to look for God's appointments and then capitalize on them.

Philip had learned to hear God's voice and to obey it. All he got was a direction; from there he simply looked for the divine appointment. When he saw this African official, the Spirit prompted him again, and Philip seized the moment. Philip entered into this man's story, answering his questions and explaining the story of Jesus. Once again, the power of story was activated, and it penetrated the man's heart with conviction. The official gave his life to Jesus and was baptized on the spot.

Increase my faith, God, in how You will use my story
and help me to enter into the stories of others.
I'm looking for today's appointment.

day 298

This is how much God loved the world: He gave his Son, his one and only Son. And this is why: so that no one need be destroyed; by believing in him, anyone can have a whole and lasting life.
John 3:16 MSG

To the Moon and Back

You have a story, but God has a story too. In fact, your story is a part of God's grand epic of pursuing love that spans the history of time. A wonderful design. An insidious plot. A daring rescue across time and space. This was a life-and-death drama that cost God everything but secured a happy ending for those who believe the story.

There's a children's story in which a daddy rabbit and his kid take turns describing how much they love each other. Each tries to outdo the other with how high and big and wide their love is. "I love you to the moon," his boy whispers sleepily. The dad murmurs back to his slumbering son, "I love you to the moon . . . and back."

How much does God love you? To the earth . . . and back.

Oh, thank You, God, for a story big enough to include me. And for a love that reaches across the chasm of separation to reunite us.

day 299

Go into all the world and preach the gospel to the whole creation.
Mark 16:15 HCSB

Commissioned Greatly

A story is made to be told, right? You can't tell your story to the entire world, but you can tell it to *your* world! This storytelling lies at the heart of the New Rebellion—the desire to live a big story and to share it where people are interested. It's the story of the King and the Kingdom. It's a story that reaches out to invite all hearers into its embrace.

This piece of the story is usually called the Great Commission, and it was Jesus' last address to His disciples. It begins with a statement of His authority and the implication that you now walk in His authority to tell His story. The address ends with His promise to be with you always, which means that the telling of His story will always be accompanied by His presence.

Make me to be a good teller of Your story, God.
Thank You that Your presence will always
empower my life and my story.

day 300

You will receive power when the Holy Spirit comes on you; and you will be my witnesses in Jerusalem, and in all Judea and Samaria, and to the ends of the earth.
Acts 1:8 NIV

Job Descriptions

God not only promises His presence when you tell His story; He promises His power! A God-sized story will bring God-sized results!

You're not alone, you know—the Holy Spirit's job is to fill you, lead you, and empower you in all of life. He will fuel the story and lead you into divine opportunities to "witness." Witnessing isn't a heavy deal. You don't have to convince anyone; that's the Spirit's role. Your role is to give your account of your personal experience with the Savior. When hearts are prepared and ready, the story will be gratefully received and honestly embraced.

The story, energized by the Spirit's presence, will multiply exponentially until it fills the earth with an eternal hope. Don't be surprised if God takes you into places as His agent of change you wouldn't expect to be.

Break off any intimidation with telling my story, God.
You are the hope of the world, and I want to
spread that hope around today.

day 301

My life is worth nothing unless I use it for doing the work assigned me by the Lord Jesus—the work of telling others the Good News about God's wonderful kindness and love.
Acts 20:24 NLT

The Meaning of Life

This was Paul's commentary on his life; is it yours? Do you find your worth and meaning in following the leading of God's Spirit? Is this the work that motivates and satisfies your soul? What can compare with a vision like that? This is the life you were made for.

You don't have to be Paul, because God has your own assignments, custom-designed for you. Don't worry about your assignments being too big for you. They're big enough to require your partnership with Him, and that's what you want anyway. In whatever line of work and whatever setting, you will have the chance to tell your experience of the good news, so don't hold back. Your story of God's kindness will change lives, and changed lives is the point of the New Rebellion. Yes, your life has tremendous worth.

God, please give me Your perspective on my life's worth. I want to live out the good news every day and everywhere!

day
302

Search me, O God, and know my heart; test me and know my anxious thoughts. See if there is any offensive way in me, and lead me in the way everlasting. Psalm 139:23–24 NIV

Transparency Is Safety

Read that verse through one more time, close your eyes, and let it sink into your soul. What emotions pop up to the surface? Does this prayer feel like a castle of refuge or a den of lions? In other words, is God a safe place for your heart?

Transparency before God is a given. He knows every complicated and contradictory facet of your soul, and His love is a white-hot passion that never dims or fades. If anyone should be a safe place for your heart, it's God. At the same time He holds you to the highest standards possible, and those truths don't seem to mesh: a God who knows your failures in excruciating detail yet loves you with infinite capacity. This must be something heavenly! Exactly.

Shakespeare got it right: "To err is human, to forgive divine."

Your capacity, God, to love me without reservation and forgive me without limitation is the single greatest joy of my life.

day 303

Confess your trespasses to one another, and pray for one another, that you may be healed. The effective, fervent prayer of a righteous man avails much.

James 5:16 NKJV

Go Public

When sin first entered the world, its first effect upon Adam and Eve was to bring guilt and separation and prompt them to hide. And that hasn't changed. Your guilt will tempt you to hide as well: to put on a mask of indifference, a pretense of happiness, or some other attempt to deceive yourself and others.

In contrast, James urges you to bring it out of hiding—to find someone you can trust and confess it to them. This level of honesty is extremely vulnerable—it's scary—but it builds a bond of friendship like little else. Together, in that place of unity and repentance, there is a power generated that rocks the spiritual realm! Your prayers at that point will be divinely effective. People are healed. Lives are changed. The Rebellion advances.

God, help me to take the risk involved to
come into that place of confession.
I know that You have taken away my shame.

day 304

If we admit our sins—make a clean
breast of them—he won't let us down;
he'll be true to himself. He'll forgive our
sins and purge us of all wrongdoing.
1 John 1:9 MSG

Double-Delete

The act of bringing your sin out of the shadows and into the light breaks the power of sin to shame you. It positions your heart for the freeing blast of forgiveness that unceasingly flows from heaven to you.

When you're working on the computer, you can always delete a file that you no longer need or that contains sensitive information. But savvy users know that it's not really gone; you can usually go to a certain directory and recover it. Sometimes you can think this way about God—*Yeah, He says He forgives me, but what if I make the same mistake again? Doesn't my guilt sort of accumulate?*

But God "double-deletes"—His forgiveness is 100 percent effective to the repentant heart. Your guilt is gone forever, and there's no recovering those files. Talk about freedom!

God, You are absolutely amazing! Thank You
for cutting off the ball and chain of past
sin and empowering me for the future.

day
305

You must make allowance for each other's faults and forgive the person who offends you. Remember, the Lord forgave you, so you must forgive others.
Colossians 3:13 NLT

Increase Your Allowance

Maybe you've heard the story Jesus told about a man who was in debtor's prison for a million-dollar loss he could never hope to repay. When the king compassionately released him from his debt, he immediately went looking for a guy who owed him a few bucks. Disregarding the pleas for mercy, he brought charges against the guy. What an absurd thing to do!

The injustice of that story strikes at the heart. You have been forgiven a debt you could never repay. Shouldn't your life now be marked by an extravagant mercy? Shouldn't it be second nature now to graciously forgive the faults and offenses of others against yourself? This is the way of the New Rebellion, and this is the way of life. Make it your goal to become a man or woman who is hard to offend.

Build in me a heart of forgiveness toward others,
God, that thrives in the ongoing joy of my own
awesome forgiveness from You.

day 306

Be kind and compassionate to one another, forgiving one another, just as God also forgave you in Christ.
Ephesians 4:32 HCSB

Receive Free, Give Free

Why did God set such a strange precedent called forgiveness? He didn't have to. After the failure of Eden, He could have just judged Adam and Eve immediately and stopped the whole human experiment. But although God is completely just, He is not defined completely by His justice. He is also shaped by an equal commitment to kindness and compassion. And being God, He is able to bring those two virtues together in His own character and in yours. This is His intention.

As ambassadors of Christ on planet Earth, it is your task to demonstrate His extraordinary capacity for forgiveness. And you'll have lots of opportunities! The lack of kindness abounds in this world, and the effects of bitterness and cynicism are rampant. They destroy the heart. But forgiveness restores the heart and ultimately transforms the world.

God, cleanse my heart from all residue of judgment, cynicism, and bitterness. Let grace flow easily and freely from my heart to all.

If you . . . suddenly remember that someone has something against you, leave your sacrifice there beside the altar. Go and be reconciled to that person. Then come and offer your sacrifice to God.

Matthew 5:23–24 NLT

day 307

The Offender

God is very serious about maintaining clear relationships within the New Rebellion community. Unresolved offenses are not an option! You do not have the luxury of nursing a grudge against any other person, regardless of the depth of injury you have sustained. When you do, you are undermining the entire community and weakening the very cause you have given your life to.

When you come into church to worship, make sure that—as far as you know—there are no broken relationships in that place. If it comes to your realization that you have given offense to another person, don't wait a moment. Go to that one and do your best to work it out. Repent for any sin you may have done against that person, even unintentionally. Cultivate a heart that finds it easy to repent and ask forgiveness.

God, it can be so hard to humble myself when I don't feel I was in the wrong. But reconciliation is worth the price of confession.

day 308

If a fellow believer hurts you, go and tell him—work it out between the two of you.
Matthew 18:15 MSG

The Offendee

Matthew's gospel hits it from both sides: If you know that someone is offended with you, then you go to him or her. If you know that you are offended with someone, then you go as well. Regardless of who did the offending, if you become aware that there is trouble in the relationship, don't wait for the other guy to initiate reconciliation. *You* take the initiative! You move in an attitude of humility and love, and see what God will do.

There are times when the other person will not extend or receive forgiveness, and that is a real loss to the cause of the Rebellion. You cannot change another person or make them do the right thing; you have responsibility for only your own heart and actions. Sometimes forgiveness is a process, so don't give up if it's not immediate.

God, I want to become an expert in forgiveness!
Quick to offer it and receive it. Quick to lay down
my "rights" to pursue reconciliation.

Some soldiers were questioning him, saying, "And what about us, what shall we do?" And he said to them, "Do not take money from anyone by force, or accuse anyone falsely, and be content with your wages."
Luke 3:14 NASB

day 309

Murmuring

The soldiers that put this question to Jesus were looking for the practical impact of the Kingdom message. They were asking, in essence, "What does a New Rebellion life look like for a first-century soldier?" To which Jesus responded—justice and contentment. Apparently, their culture as soldiers was overrun with corruption and discontent, and these forces were at complete odds with the Kingdom Jesus was bringing.

Two thousand years later, it is still human nature to take what you have for granted and to envy those who have more. It rises up easily in the human heart to murmur and complain about your place in life. But a Kingdom perspective gives rise to a grateful and contented heart, which positions you to go after the things that really matter—Spiritual goals must take priority over material goals.

I really want to honor You, God, with the contentment that secures my heart and keeps me focused on what's really important.

day 310

Godliness with contentment is a great gain.
For we brought nothing into the world,
and we can take nothing out.
1 Timothy 6:6–7 HCSB

Not All That Glitters Is Gold

Sometimes people confuse contentment with apathy or fatalism. But it is neither. You can be very ambitious and motivated in life at the same time that you are content. The difference lies in focus. Worldly ambition focuses upon material gain and personal power. Godly ambition focuses upon spiritual gain and God's power. The world focuses upon temporary pleasures while the New Rebellion focuses upon eternal ones. Pleasures that begin now and last forever.

Contentment requires trust and faith—trust in God's commitment to provide all the natural resources you need and faith that the unseen is more real than the seen. Kingdom eyes see what is truly valuable—intimate relationships, using your spiritual gifts, prayer and worship, and so forth. Today, you can rest completely in the circumstances God has placed you in and at the same time, pursue godliness with great ambition.

God, bring those two dimensions into harmony in my life this day—the pursuit of godliness along with an abiding contentment.

Not that I was ever in need, for I have learned how to get along happily whether I have much or little. I know how to live on almost nothing or with everything.
Philippians 4:11–12 NLT

day 311

Absolute Freedom

Can you feel the liberation that Paul lived with? Because he could roll with the changes that life brought, he was unstoppable. There was no circumstance that could defeat him. But this attitude doesn't come naturally for many; it is a mind-set forged in the New Rebellion.

Most people are encouraged when their outer conditions are going well and they experience abundance; on the flip side, when circumstances change and they encounter great difficulty, discouragement rises. Everyone can relate to that. But that is natural thinking, and it will cloud your effectiveness as a Rebel. When you are most energized by the relationships and activities of the Kingdom, then you realize that you can be effective in those regardless of your material status. This doesn't mean that God isn't interested in your natural provision; His blessings impact every facet of life.

Make me that solid and unshakable, God, where my heart can be happily content both when everything is going great and when it isn't.

day 312

Your life should be free from the love of money. Be satisfied with what you have, for He Himself has said, "I will never leave you or forsake you."
Hebrews 13:5 HCSB

Free Is Good!

Money is a powerful motivator, and of course, money serves a necessary purpose. But the love of money is a recipe for disaster! And God's point is that you don't have to be driven by that motivation any longer; you're free if you choose to be.

Freedom enters your heart through the realization that you already possess the most priceless gift of all—God Himself. He will never leave you, and you can never get rid of Him. There is no failure or circumstance that can drive God from you; you belong to Him. You're family!

The riches you now possess through Christ are what bring satisfaction to every life situation. Money is no longer the source of your security or identity; Jesus is. Money is not your hope for the future; Jesus is. And that is a reason for contentment.

God, You are everything I need and everything I could imagine wanting. Now I can lead a life of purpose and contentment.

There is one alone, without companion: he has neither son nor brother. Yet there is no end to all his labors, nor is his eye satisfied with riches. But he never asks, "For whom do I toil and deprive myself of good?" This also is vanity and a grave misfortune.
Ecclesiastes 4:8 NKJV

day
313

Misspent Effort

The opposite of contentment isn't ambition; it's disillusionment.

The discontent are driven to labor endlessly, and the real tragedy of it is that they don't know what will really satisfy them. And so they don't know what to pursue or how to obtain it; they simply toil on, heedless of the simple pleasures that surround them, and destined to frustration. That's not a road you want to be on. "A grave misfortune," Ecclesiastes calls it.

But the content are at rest internally even while they work externally. Their work is motivated by love, not lack. They invest themselves in people and so there is always someone to double their joys and share their sorrows. They know when to stop working and enjoy the fruit of their labor. They are satisfied now and are assured of more to come.

This is the quality of life I'm looking for, God. Anchor my soul in a deep, abiding contentment in You and enjoyment of life.

day 314

If my people would but listen to me . . . you would be
fed with the finest of wheat; with honey
from the rock I would satisfy you.
Psalm 81:13, 16 NIV

An Attentive Heart—A Satisfied Heart

If there is one quality that captures the essence of God, it is *goodness*. He cannot be anything other than good. Although evil has a place in this world, it has no place in Him. This means that you will experience some bad things in life but only good from His hand. Which is a good reason to listen closely to His voice and obey Him with great attention.

If this is the course you chart, your life will be an ongoing testimony to the extravagant goodness of God. You may not be rich in dollars, but your every need will find an abundant provision. And this experience will qualify you as an effective Rebel—people will see the good news in your life even before they hear it from your mouth. Your satisfaction in Him will change the world significantly.

Make my life a constant witness to the grace and kindness of Your hand, God. You satisfy my every desire with good things!

Because your love is better than life, my lips will glorify you. I will praise you as long as I live, and in your name I will lift up my hands. My soul will be satisfied as with the richest of foods; with singing lips my mouth will praise you.
Psalm 63:3–5 NIV

God Goes Gourmet

Contentment is closely connected to praise and worship. Did you know that? A contented heart is a grateful heart, recognizing the source of all good things. Gratitude leads you to remind yourself and others of all the amazing things God has done. Whether it's in church on Sunday or on the telephone Monday, praise is your testimony to the character and deeds of God, your acknowledgment that He is eternally good. To you and to all.

This expression of praise naturally leads you into worship—into an intimate connection with the Savior, expressing your undying love and delight in Him and receiving His even greater joy in you. This contented joy will always be a wonder to those seeking the New Rebellion, and will open many doors of opportunity for you. They are looking for satisfaction, and you hold the answer!

Make my contentment contagious, God. Let me be an authentic voice for declaring Your goodness to seekers wherever I go.

day 316

The Spirit of the Lord GOD is upon me, because the LORD has anointed me to bring good news to the afflicted; He has sent me to bind up the brokenhearted, to proclaim liberty to captives and freedom to prisoners.
Isaiah 61:1 NASB

Mission: Possible

Seven hundred years before Jesus was born as a man, the prophet Isaiah described the ministry of the Messiah: The Spirit of God would fill Him, He would bring a message of hope, He would comfort the distressed, and He would liberate those who were held prisoner by sin and death. It was a tall order. And it was long in the coming.

But for year after year, generation after generation, this promise was kept alive until finally, when many had stopped looking, Messiah appeared! The impossible mission was finally accomplished; freedom was won at great cost. But it's not over yet; the New Rebellion carries that same mission forward—bringing that same message and comfort and liberty to each new generation. You carry on His mission! You are an agent of the Messiah. Your life is messianic.

I do choose to accept this mission.
I will be Your agent on planet Earth.
Today, I will bring hope and freedom to my world.

day
317

Christ has set us free to live a free life. So take your stand! Never again let anyone put a harness of slavery on you. I am emphatic about this.
Galatians 5:1–2 MSG

Jailbreak

Imagine for a moment that you are back in the Old West, when justice was slow and guns were quick. Your best friend has been falsely imprisoned by the local strongman, and you're going to bust him out. The guards are lured away, the jail is jimmied, and the door swings open, but your friend just stands there. "Nope," he says, "I'm just fine here." What?!

Jesus made the impossible rescue, opening your jail cell of guilt and inviting you into lasting freedom. Why would you ever willingly go back when you own the deed to a mansion? But every time you choose to sin, you're clapping the irons back on yourself. Every time you try to earn God's favor by trying hard, you put yourself behind bars. Once you receive the grace of God, don't ever let it go.

Thank You for the precious gift of freedom, God.
I'm going to vigilantly protect that freedom from
every enemy within and without.

day 318

Let me ask you this one question: Did you receive the Holy Spirit by keeping the law? Of course not, for the Holy Spirit came upon you only after you believed the message you heard about Christ. Have you lost your senses? After starting your Christian lives in the Spirit, why are you now trying to become perfect by your own human effort?
Galatians 3:2–3 NLT

God Trumps Your Efforts at Performance

The drive to prove yourself goes deep. The effect of sin upon the soul is to be driven by fear and pulled by pride to take care of yourself. To be independent and self-sufficient. But that gets you nowhere fast.

Contemporary culture fans the flame of performance by assigning value to people according to what they can produce. So when you come into the Kingdom, there is a long-term pattern of performance-driven relationship to overcome.

God cuts to the root of that motivation by declaring that you can never do enough to get free, and you don't have to! He has performed for you and given you the reward. So come back to your senses! Quit trying to do the right things for the wrong reasons. Your obedience must flow from the security of salvation by grace alone.

I know it in my head, God, so help me walk it out in daily life—serving You as the expression of my love, not to earn Yours.

Those who cling to worthless idols forfeit the grace that could be theirs. But I, with a song of thanksgiving, will sacrifice to you. What I have vowed I will make good. Salvation comes from the LORD.
Jonah 2:8–9 NIV

day 319

Idols Enslave

It's easy to think that the age of idolatry is long gone since few bow down to carved figures of wood and stone these days. But that would be a big mistake.

An idol is anything that takes the central place of Christ in your heart. Anything that motivates your behavior or captures your affection more than Him. Modern-day idols include entertainment, time management, physical beauty, work, and hobbies. While each of these things has its appropriate place in your life, that place is not the throne. Pretty much everyone falls into this trap at times, and when you do, the grace that your soul rightly craves gets strangled as you forfeit your freedom in Christ.

The prophet Jonah learned this the hard way after a three-day/three-night vacation inside a whale. The result: a fresh appetite for grace.

God, keep me grateful for grace and far from the many counterfeits that want to enslave me through idolatry. Freedom comes only from You.

day 320

By grace you are saved through faith, and this is not from yourselves; it is God's gift—not from works, so that no one can boast.
Ephesians 2:8–9 HCSB

The Gift That Keeps on Giving

Grace is that amazing event where you are given something that you don't even begin to deserve. You catch fragments of grace in this world—someone lets you step in line ahead of them or a cashier offers you a coupon as you're getting ready to pay full price. Even little moments like that warm the heart with a heavenly fire. But it's in your relationship with God where you stand to lose the most and have the most to gain.

God's grace comes free but is activated by faith—by recognizing your dependency upon Him and His sufficiency for you. And it's a gift that doesn't just happen once. God's grace is meant to be your daily experience of receiving many things you could never buy: wisdom, confidence, healing, courage, you name it! His grace never quits.

I'm looking for a fresh deposit of grace today,
God. You know what I need and how to lead
me into new measures of freedom.

day 321

All that passing laws against sin did was produce more lawbreakers. But sin didn't, and doesn't, have a chance in competition with the aggressive forgiveness we call grace. When it's sin versus grace, grace wins hands down.
Romans 5:20 MSG

Sin Gets KO'd

Yes, God is aggressive in grace. He's gone head-to-head with sin and won. And you're the beneficiary! Sin will no longer have bragging rights over you; you're forgiven. But grace is more than forgiveness, more than just the elimination of a debt or threat; grace is the power of God given to you to become the woman or man He designed you to be. Grace restores your destiny and places you in the winner's circle.

Now when sin tries to rear its ugly head again—and it will—you have the power to take him down. Grace will always conquer your fears, defeat your pride, and overcome your greed. Through grace, you become a partner with heaven and a world-changer. When life feels threatening and dangerous, find your place in the grace of God and relax. You're the threat now!

Yes, God, I believe that. Through Your grace, my life is a dangerous threat to the enemy, and I will triumph over sin today.

day 322

He who testifies to these things says, "Surely I am coming quickly." Amen. Even so, come, Lord Jesus! The grace of our Lord Jesus Christ be with you all. Amen
Revelation 22:20–21 NKJV

Over and Out

These are the closing words of Scripture—the final statement of God's written word to the church. Jesus promised that His return is near. Two thousand years may not feel terribly "near," and yet His Kingdom and His rule are advanced by the New Rebellion daily. And when the time is right, He will come in person to bring the final liberation to planet Earth.

In response to this promise, the apostle John says two things: *Come, Lord, we're eagerly waiting!* and *Keep yourselves in the grace of God*. The grace is there for you; now live in it and own it and never let it go. John's words are a benediction, a blessing, an affirmation, and an impartation. He is confirming the greatest reality we could imagine—that we are truly reinstated as heirs of heaven and coworkers with God Himself.

How could I ever thank You adequately for the gift of grace, God? I will keep myself immersed in it all the days of my life.

day
323

I'm not asking that you take them out of the world
but that you guard them from the Evil One. They
are no more defined by the world than I am
defined by the world. Make them holy—
consecrated—with the truth.
John 17:15–17 MSG

In but Not Of

The New Rebellion exists to advance the Kingdom of God in the earth. It is a movement destined to impact every facet of society, from individuals to families to churches to cities to nations. It spans neighborhoods and businesses and governments. God intends His people to be "salt" and "light" (see Matthew 5:13–14)—a preserving, flavoring, and illuminating influence upon society.

Your job is to be "in, but not of." In other words, you live *in* the world but you are not *of* the world. You are *of* the Kingdom of heaven, operating under its rules and its agenda. It's a tall order, but Jesus has prayed—and does pray—for your constant success. He will guard you from the enemy, both the schemes of Satan and your own flesh. He will purify your motivations and empower you with His truth.

God, help me to confidently enter into many dimensions of this culture, bringing Your life and love into every place I go.

day 324

[If] My people who are called by My name humble themselves and pray and seek My face and turn from their wicked ways, then I will hear from heaven, will forgive their sin and will heal their land.
2 Chronicles 7:14 NASB

Lift!

God is in the business of hearing, forgiving, and healing, but He's looking for people who will ask! People who carry both the humility and the vision to intercede for their land.

Part of being in the Rebellion is not putting up with the status quo but believing for change! Revolution, in fact. And so God looks for those who will carry His vision for restoration and who will do something about it—pray for their land!

So what is your "land"? Your land is what belongs to you, what you carry in your heart and care about and pray for. Your vision may be for your neighborhood; if so, pray for God's healing there! If your vision is for your city, then pray God's redemption into your city. Maybe you burn for the entire world—God intends to heal that as well!

I'm humbling my heart before You, O God, and asking You today to hear these prayers, to forgive and heal those I hold before Your throne.

Pure and lasting religion in the sight of God our Father means that we must care for orphans and widows in their troubles, and refuse to let the world corrupt us.
James 1:27 NLT

day 325

Advocacy

What does it mean to let the world corrupt you? In this context, James implies that there is progressive influence upon you to neglect the needy and defenseless. The world accomplishes this through busyness, a judgmental spirit, or apathy and complacency. Whatever may be the methods for dulling compassion, it arouses God's anger! He says, in effect, *Don't even bother calling yourself a Christian if you aren't giving out in some form to those less fortunate than yourself.*

This verse also raises the question: Who's affecting who? In what direction is the influence flowing? If the world and its values are shaping who you are, then you are in the process of being corrupted. God's intent is that His life within you would be so contagious, so radiant with hope and mercy, that it can't help but influence your world.

God, I want to be the influencer, demonstrating a pure and holy passion for You by serving those who are overlooked and helpless.

day 326

You have insulted the poor. Is it not the rich who are exploiting you? . . . But if you show favoritism, you sin and are convicted by the law as lawbreakers.
James 2:6, 9 NIV

Our Favorite Sin

The sin that is perhaps most native to your humanity is basic selfishness. One form is favoritism—showing attention to those who can give something valuable back to you. It may be most ugly when you give friendship in exchange for power or influence or financial reward, but pretty much everyone bestows friendship in exchange for the enjoyment of someone else's company.

This isn't a bad thing, per se. But it's not enough, according to James. The poor and needy aren't usually able to offer you anything that would build your reputation or status in the world, but they can give you gratitude and sometimes friendship. And then there are times when you help someone and get nothing at all in return or maybe even hostility. This is the quality of love that drives the New Rebellion and the Kingdom!

God, I want to love people with a depth and endurance of love that reflects Yours, especially those who have nothing to give back.

day
327

What good is it, my brothers, if someone says he has faith, but does not have works? Can his faith save him?
James 2:14 HCSB

Faith Works

When the apostolic letters of the New Testament were being evaluated and compiled, there was some controversy over whether James should be admitted, basically because of his emphasis upon faith in action. In contrast, Paul emphasized the grace of God that could never be earned by spiritual activity. But it was true then as it is true now that both truths are essential to the Christian life: faith is a free gift, and faith will always show itself in action.

When people say, "My faith is personal," what they usually mean is that it has no effect upon anyone else, which really means that it has no effect upon them. But faith is not supposed to be a secret! The activity of faith is meant to have an impact upon the world! It begins personally but quickly transitions to affecting society.

I want to make a difference, God. I want my life and my faith to have impact upon the culture and society I live within.

day 328

Let the fear of the LORD be upon you. Judge carefully, for with the LORD our God there is no injustice or partiality or bribery.
2 Chronicles 19:7 NIV

Pray for Peace, Work for Justice

There's a bumper sticker that reads: "Pray for peace, work for justice." This is a godly mission, reflecting the kind of partnership God calls you to within the New Rebellion. You pray for God to do the things only He can do, and in this way, you come into agreement and release His purposes across the world. Then you work—in whatever type of employment God has placed you in—with the conviction that God will empower you to bring blessing and justice through your labors.

This level of holy partnership requires the fear of the Lord. You don't work in your own strength and you don't pray in your own wisdom. It is only out of a deep and pervasive respect for the will of God that you enter into partnership with Him, knowing that together, you are unstoppable!

God, cause me to know the just designs of Your will and then pray and work accordingly, believing that we will change the world.

day 329

Which of these three do you think was neighbor to him who fell among the thieves?
Luke 10:36 NKJV

The Long Reach

Do you remember the story of the good Samaritan? After a Jewish traveler is robbed and injured by bandits, three men pass by him as he lies in the ditch. The first two were Jewish religious leaders—the ones anyone would expect to help the needy, but they looked the other way and hurried along. The third to pass was a man from Samaria, a region hated by the Jews, yet he bandaged up the traveler's wounds and carried him to an inn for recovery.

It's easy to turn away from the less fortunate in your world; the sum of pain and suffering can feel overwhelming! But as the Samaritan showed, you only have to help one person at a time. Make a difference today by living out the Kingdom call in a way that aids another person who has less than you do.

Give me eyes to see the hurting, God, and a willingness to be inconvenienced for the opportunity to serve someone in need.

day 330

God anointed Jesus of Nazareth with the Holy Spirit and power, and . . . he went around doing good and healing all who were under the power of the devil, because God was with him.
Acts 10:38 NIV

The Template

The New Rebellion is about walking in the same anointing as Jesus and doing the same things He did. The same Holy Spirit that filled Jesus now fills you—that is some pretty amazing power flowing through you! So let it flow. The good that you see to do, do it. Those who need healing, heal them in the name of Jesus. God was with Jesus, and God is with you.

The New Rebellion is about setting people free from the power of the devil. This means that you can't be intimidated by him; you have to know your authority and anointing are greater than his. God intends to replicate the works of Jesus through you—this is the clear, consistent message of the gospel. You aren't a well-intentioned bystander; you are a Kingdom warrior!

I'm ready to be Your channel of hope and healing in my world, God. Show me who and how You want to heal today.

"What do you want Me to do for you?" And he said, "Lord, I want to regain my sight!" And Jesus said to him, "Receive your sight; your faith has made you well."
Luke 18:41 NASB

day 331

Wanting What God Wants

Most of the times Scripture records Jesus healing people, there is some reference to faith. Simply put, faith activates miracles. And while faith may feel intimidating, the good news is that faith is not complicated at all. It's not about being personally powerful; it's about recognizing God's power. Faith is aligning yourself with the will of God; when you and God come into agreement, power is released.

God's Kingdom Rebels bring Kingdom life wherever they go. Kingdom life was lived out perfectly in the Garden of Eden, and though the world is no longer perfect, God is still in the business of restoring health, restoring intimacy, and restoring community that reflects the Garden. Don't be so quick to just accept sickness when heaven wants to show up in the miraculous. Rebel against fatalism and choose life!

Renew my sight, God, with a vision for faith and healing. Help me to see what You're doing and join You in miracles large and small.

day 332

The person who trusts me will not only do what I'm doing but even greater things, because I, on my way to the Father, am giving you the same work to do that I've been doing.
John 14:12 MSG

Passing the Baton

It stretches the imagination that you would do the same things in your world that Jesus did in His. But as if that weren't enough, He upped the ante! "Even greater things," Jesus said, is what you can look forward to doing if you're willing to reach beyond normal. Willing to trust big and reach big. Will that be you? Will you accept the same assignment that Jesus had when He came to earth?

Miracles can be defined as good things that happen outside the norm. Beyond average expectation. But when you're in the New Rebellion, your expectations change! Suddenly, the more you believe God can do, the more He does. Miracles begin to happen, and "normal" is redefined. This is where Kingdom living gets exciting: trusting God to bring His extraordinary healing of body and soul to the people in your world.

I want to live beyond "normal," God. I want to look for the Kingdom to break into people's lives and bring healing everywhere.

day
333

A spiritual gift is given to each of us as a means of helping the entire church . . . The Spirit gives special faith to another, and to someone else he gives the power to heal the sick.
1 Corinthians 12:7, 9 NLT

Specialists

Anyone can pray and ask God to heal, but some are given a special spiritual gift: the Holy Spirit inside them wants to bring healing to sick people. Cool, huh?

There are lots of spiritual gifts, so how do you know which is yours? By asking, praying, and experimenting. "Earnestly desire spiritual gifts," Paul urges his readers two chapters later. This isn't really a suggestion; this is a command! And it honors God when you desire the gifts He offers.

When you think you have an idea of your spiritual gift, take a risk and try something to see what God will do. If you have a desire to see folks healed, pray for sick people. Lots of them! Don't give up if you're not immediately successful; let God train you and release the gift He's placed inside you.

I'm willing to take a risk, God. Help me to trust You, pray, and look for You to heal the people I pray for.

day
334

He heals the brokenhearted
and binds up their wounds.
Psalm 147:3 NIV

Soul Repair

God is not only a Warrior, He's also a Shepherd. And as a Shepherd, He brings healing and wholeness to every soul who comes to Him. He has healed you and made you a healer of others.

Emotional healing is just as (and sometimes more) important than physical healing. God wants you to be healthy in every facet of your body, your spirit, your mind, and your emotions. Many people suffer in their emotions, bearing the effects of past sins for many years. That's not God's design. He intends to pull the poison out of old wounds so they no longer have any destructive power in your life.

Sometimes your healing is tied to your forgiveness—that is, to your forgiving others who have sinned against you. If you can think of any resentments hanging around, deal with them today through forgiveness.

God, I receive Your power to heal my heart as well as my body. Now make me someone who can bring Your healing to others.

day 335

They went out and preached that people should repent. And they were driving out many demons, anointing many sick people with oil, and healing.

Mark 6:12–13 HCSB

A Logical Progression

In the New Rebellion, Jesus' disciples are given authority over all the works of the enemy. As you bring the love of Jesus to people you meet today, they may be in different places of need. Some are crushed by guilt; some are tormented by demons; some need healing from sickness. And God will use you to bring hope to each situation!

This verse does reflect a progression, however. Repentance is the act where Satan's authority to bring guilt and oppression is broken. This is the beginning of salvation and establishes the rule of Christ within the heart of a person. Once this step is taken, then you have authority to drive out any demons that would like to stick around and continue robbing the person. God's authority, along with their agreement, sets them free. Then they're ready for physical healing.

I will be an instrument of liberation for people today, God. Through Your power, I will lead them to repentance, freedom, and health.

day 336

A thorn in the flesh was given to me, a messenger of Satan to torment me so I would not exalt myself. Concerning this, I pleaded with the Lord three times to take it away from me. But He said to me, "My grace is sufficient for you."
2 Corinthians 12:7–9 HCSB

God's in Charge

In your work as God's Rebel, you may encounter situations where God does not intend to immediately heal someone. This is not, obviously, because He lacks the power to do it, or because He lacks the will to bless that person. It's precisely because of His commitment to people's blessing that He will occasionally allow an ailment for a specific purpose—because He wants to give the person a fresh revelation of His character that, at that moment, is more important than their healing.

Paul experienced this very dynamic. The affliction itself is not clear in Scripture, but his desire to be free of it is. Nevertheless, Jesus denied his request in order to give him a whole new experience of the surpassing grace of God that enables God's kids to endure suffering from a place of sufficient provision.

This is my inheritance too, God—the experience of grace to endure suffering when it's not Your purpose to heal. You are always good!

day 337

"I know the plans that I have for you," declares the LORD, "plans for welfare and not for calamity to give you a future and a hope. Then you will call upon Me and come and pray to Me, and I will listen to you. You will seek Me and find Me when you search for Me with all your heart."

Jeremiah 29:11–13 NASB

Back to the Future

If there is one thing about God that faces constant fire from the enemy, it's your assurance of His unceasing goodness toward you. And so to spell it out in indisputable clarity, God spoke to the prophet Jeremiah that His plans for His people are for blessing. He offers you reason to hope, reason to believe that your future will be full of goodness. Without this conviction, your life will be aimless at best, devastated at worst.

Because God has good plans for you, you can afford to seek those plans out. He invites you to draw close and inquire of Him; He promises to listen and answer! But are you catching the pattern? The finding is preceded by the seeking. God will never be a machine where you drop in your dollar and out comes the answer; He requires relationship.

God, to be invited into relationship with You is the most astounding opportunity ever. From that holy place, I trust You to lead me.

day 338

Oh, that my steps might be steady, keeping to the course you set; then I'd never have any regrets in comparing my life with your counsel.
Psalm 119:5–6 MSG

No Regrets

When God's kids look to their heavenly Father for guidance, it satisfies His heart in an amazing way. It communicates so much—dependency upon a greater wisdom, trust in a loving hand, and desire for partnership in the quest of life. Every time you direct your attention to heaven and sincerely ask for God's guidance, His heart rejoices and responds with all you need to know.

It can be a challenge, however, to hear the responses of God in the midst of the "head noise" of your own anxiety and other voices. This calls for patience and the skills that develop over time. The psalmist expressed his yearning for that heavenly counsel, implicitly acknowledging that there were times he had missed it. But because his heart was set upon God over the long haul, he lived a life of few regrets!

Hear my heart's cry, God. Keep me from missing the mark and sustain me when I do so that I can return to the source of wisdom.

You guide me with your counsel, and afterward you will take me into glory. Whom have I in heaven but you? And earth has nothing I desire besides you.
Psalm 73:24–25 NIV

day 339

Heaven Inbound

Asaph was the author of this passionate cry of consecration: "God, You are everything to me," he declares. "In the entire universe, there is nothing so valuable, so constant in my affection, as You!" Does that resonate within your heart? Is His favor, His direction, His fellowship your supreme pursuit?

This man was Israel's greatest worship leader, and his view of life was very simple: Being actively led by God through the maze of this world and finally led into a glorious eternity with God Himself. Asaph's many hours leading worship seem to have impressed him deeply with the nearness of God and God's dedication to his guidance.

You, too, can trust the Father's heart to guide you with good counsel in the perplexing circumstances you face. God's counsel directs the Rebellion, and His counsel will direct your life.

You are the center, the target of my life, God. I look for Your wise counsel in the decisions I'll make today. Open my ears to hear.

day 340

GOD is fair and just, he corrects the misdirected, sends them in the right direction. He gives the rejects his hand, and leads them step-by-step.
Psalm 25:8–9 MSG

Hope for Rejects

Are you a reject? Every person has experienced a certain amount of hostility and rejection from others; it's part of sin's effect to separate people and damage relationships. And if you have given your life to the New Rebellion, it's just a matter of time before you will experience some rejection for your life's pursuit. Those who reject God will reject you; Jesus said as much (see Matthew 10:22).

Just as much as rejection from some in the world is a foregone conclusion, so acceptance from God is your birthright. And His acceptance brings a wholehearted commitment to your future. He will take your hand and lead you step-by-step in the right direction. You can count on it! He never tires of redirecting your path. He never gets fed up with your mistakes or gives up on you.

Thank You, God, for Your loving persistence with me and for constantly bringing me back to the center of Your will. You are my Shepherd.

I guide you in the way of wisdom and lead you along straight paths. When you walk, your steps will not be hampered; when you run, you will not stumble.
Proverbs 4:11–12 NIV

day
341

Running Free

Every soul yearns to run free through life, unhampered by enemies and obstacles. This is the imprint of heaven upon the human heart, and although you live far from that paradise, you know what you're made for. The extent to which that freedom can mark your earthly journey is determined by the degree of blessing you walk in. As a child of heaven, every blessing belongs to you, but you have to learn how to obtain it.

Living in the blessings of God is a matter of attention, obedience, and faith. You have to *listen* to hear the voice of wisdom, letting God guide you through an obedient heart. Faith activates the promises of God and keeps you positioned on the right path, even when you encounter difficulties. Then you will find God opening up straight, unhindered paths for you to run.

This day I'm embracing my freedom as a Kingdom Rebel—
I'm looking and listening for the guidance of heaven
in my circumstances today.

day 342

A man's steps are directed by the LORD. How then can anyone understand his own way?
Proverbs 20:24 NIV

Making Sense of Ourselves

No woman or man fully understands their own heart or their own decisions. To be sure, you know some of your strengths and weaknesses, some of your desires and goals. But how much of that comes from your own sensibilities, how much comes from the world around you, and how much comes from the Lord?

Well, as a child of God, His promise to you is that He will direct you. He will place His desires within your heart. You're no robot; He will not override your will. But when you surrender your will to His leadership, you begin to enter into that glorious partnership where you and God are working together, bringing your will and agreement into harmony with His direction. And that's a beautiful thing. From that place, you will begin to make sense of yourself and of God.

Take control of me, dear God. I want Your hands,
not my own, on the steering wheel of my life.
You alone are trustworthy.

It came to pass in those days that He went out to the mountain to pray, and continued all night in prayer to God. And when it was day, He called His disciples to Himself; and from them He chose twelve whom He also named apostles.
Luke 6:12–13 NKJV

day 343

Case Study: Jesus

Even Jesus required the guidance of His Father in order to fulfill His mission. And as an example to you, He showed how He found guidance when He needed it. His deep relationship with the Father led Him to spend a great deal of time with Him. Even when His body was weary, as it surely was that night, His soul was refreshed in that beloved presence. And out of that communion, He found the wisdom He needed.

The Father gave Him direction to multiply His ministry—no longer would it just be Him doing the healing and preaching and caring. Now it was Jesus times twelve! The Rebellion was spreading, and now it includes you. So you, if you want to move in the authority of Jesus, will find the same direction in the same intimacy with your Father.

I'm coming close to You now, God. In our times together, speak Your truth and wisdom to me. Guide me in Your good purposes today.

day 344

Whatever you do, do your work heartily, as for the Lord rather than for men, knowing that from the Lord you will receive the reward of the inheritance. It is the Lord Christ whom you serve.
Colossians 3:23–24 NASB

The Perspective

You spend the bulk of your life in some combination of work and rest. The *way* in which you work and rest will determine the quality of your life. In the Rebellion, work is embraced as an opportunity to serve God and men, even menial work. Jesus consistently hinted at the reversed perspective of the Kingdom: "The last shall be first." But whether you're a politician or an electrician or a mathematician, you do your work as unto God.

In the Rebellion, you also know when to cease from your labors and to rest. You are vividly aware that both are holy endeavors, reflecting the very character of God. God works, you work. God rests, you rest. As a servant of heaven, you rebel against the world's warped view of work and rest and live out the beauty of heaven's rhythms.

God, You are my real "boss," and I'm determined to work well and rest well as a demonstration of heaven's rhythm here on earth.

This should be your ambition: to live a quiet life, minding your own business and working with your hands, just as we commanded you before. As a result, people who are not Christians will respect the way you live, and you will not need to depend on others to meet your financial needs.
1 Thessalonians 4:11–12 NLT

day 345

The Respect

The apostle Paul had very strong feelings about work and financial sustainability. In his own ministry, he was determined to never rely upon the means of others for his own sustenance. "If anyone does not provide for his relatives," he tells Timothy, "he has denied the faith and is worse than an unbeliever" (1 Timothy 5:8 NIV). Yet at the same time, he commended those who gave to needy churches and individuals.

In other words, Paul recognized that anyone can fall upon hard times and have genuine needs. But he also expected men and women to be diligent in supporting their own families. As you pursue the Rebellion, be equally industrious, using the skills God's given you to be prosperous and generous. This is part of earning respect for the name of Christ and validating the message that you bring.

God, give me wisdom to know how to put my abilities to good use and support myself and my family for Your honor.

day 346

The rich man had to admire the dishonest rascal for being so shrewd. And it is true that the citizens of this world are more shrewd than the godly are.
Luke 16:8 NLT

The Wisdom

In one of Jesus' stories, a man of little overall character earned commendation from God for looking ahead and making financial provision for himself. Jesus used this as an opportunity to describe a problem of naïveté that was affecting His followers. In their zeal for the things of the Kingdom, many of them were neglecting the natural requirements of the earth. Perhaps they felt that financial planning was unspiritual, compared with preaching and healing the multitudes.

But Jesus spoke to this in an effort to bring balance to their perspective: *Yes, the Kingdom is your ultimate reality, but the Kingdom includes being faithful to your natural obligations*. He wanted to see His followers exercise financial wisdom, taking responsibility for their families and for underwriting Kingdom activities. Money is meant to serve the interests of God.

God, give me a holy "shrewdness" that sees down the road and plans accordingly for the needs of my family and the cause of Christ.

day 347

Observe the Sabbath day, to keep it holy. Work six days and do everything you need to do. But the seventh day is a Sabbath to GOD, your God.
Exodus 20:8–10 MSG

The Space

Out of the famous Ten Commandments, God actually used more words to describe His vision for the Sabbath than for any of the other nine. Not only that, He modeled the pattern of work followed by rest (as if He needed rest) by creating the earth in six days and taking the seventh for rest. There must be something very important to be learned here!

Rest is a gift, a blessing that all wise sons and daughters receive with gratitude. It is practical, allowing you the chance to renew your strength—physically, mentally, emotionally, and spiritually—before reengaging with your God-given work. But more than that, rest is a statement of faith and dependency upon God: It declares that you are not self-sufficient, but that you are just a partner in God's conquest to reclaim earth.

Bring me into that great partnership with You, God, where I can rest knowing that Your work will be fully accomplished in its proper time.

day 348

Come to me, all you who are weary and burdened, and I will give you rest. Take my yoke upon you and learn from me, for I am gentle and humble in heart, and you will find rest for your souls. For my yoke is easy and my burden is light.
Matthew 11:28–30 NIV

The Refreshment

Jesus entered a world driven by relentless demands and burdens, and in two thousand years, not much has changed. People are still busy and weary and desperate for soul-rest!

Into that yearning, the life and message of Jesus fell like a cool drink of water onto parched tongues. It's not that people didn't still have a living to make, but people came to see that there was hope for change—that a soul-deep rest from all their labors to please God was finally at hand. A Savior had literally appeared and, rather than piling on the duties and obligations of religion, He offered to carry their burdens. He offered relationship. He offered Himself.

Your message of a world-changing hope is no different. You, too, come to busy, weary people and offer them respite in the form of a relationship with the Savior.

God, help me live the hope of rest in a weary world and become the message that so many are desperate to hear. Today begins anew.

day 349

A Sabbath rest remains, therefore, for God's people. For the person who has entered His rest has rested from his own works, just as God did from His.
Hebrews 4:9–10 HCSB

The Revelation

This passage in Hebrews connects the dots. The Sabbath was a foreshadowing of the rest that Christ would bring. The promised land of Israel was another picture of God's rest—a rest they turned down under Moses but received under Joshua forty years later (see Hebrews 3–4). But Jesus ultimately became the rest for every seeking soul; He is the reason that your life is no longer driven by law but led by grace. *He* is your rest!

So many people come to Jesus and find that wonderful rest only to return to a life of frantic drivenness. Yes, they are going to heaven and look forward to an eternal rest, but God's plan is to bring heaven to earth. And your job as a Rebel is to set a new standard of inner rest in the midst of this world's craziness.

God, I choose to enter into the daily rest You offer me. I will not be seduced by the world's drivenness but will revel in Your gift.

day 350

My soul finds rest in God alone; my salvation comes from him. He alone is my rock and my salvation; he is my fortress, I will never be shaken.
Psalm 62:1–2 NIV

The Worship

Worship arises from the soul at rest. Only duty rises from the driven soul.

Salvation is the source of your rest. And although your salvation began the moment you made Christ King of your life, your every day is a journey toward the fullness of salvation. God is continuously saving you from the destructive patterns of sin. Sin is the enemy of rest. Sin promises the world but delivers a taskmaster and a whip.

Rest is your inheritance. Safety. Security. Contentment. Your world may fall apart—your job, your friends, even your family may desert you. But your restful worship of God can secure your heart and empower your future. The New Rebellion is a violent revolution against the spiritual forces of hell; ironically, it is fought by those who have learned the secret of rest. Have you?

The priceless gift of rest will always cause my heart to swell in worship and adoration of Your unspeakable worth and kindness.

day 351

I will put enmity between you and the woman, and between your offspring and hers; he will crush your head, and you will strike his heel.
Genesis 3:15 NIV

The War Begins

As a follower of Jesus, your destiny is tied to His. This week contemplate the mission He undertook, and your place now in that mission.

After Jesus' role in the creation of the world, He shows up in the Father's promise that Eve would have a descendant who would crush Satan's head. Sin had destroyed paradise; the free fellowship and easy intimacy between God and humanity was broken. But hope was not lost! The seeds of a promised redemption were planted as the Father cursed the enemy, cursed the ground, and delivered a solemn set of consequences to the first couple.

Thus the war between heaven and earth entered full swing as Satan attempted to seduce men and women away from their heavenly roots. Meanwhile, a lineage of God-seekers emerged with Noah, Abraham, Isaac, Jacob, Joseph, and the rest. The promise of a Redeemer was cherished within their hearts. That lineage comes to you—a new keeper and carrier of the promise. A new Rebel.

Thank You, God, that I can share Your redemptive role—
inviting people I know past their brokenness to
the life of love You promise.

day 352

A green Shoot will sprout from Jesse's stump, from his roots a budding Branch. The life-giving Spirit of GOD will hover over him, the Spirit that brings wisdom and understanding, the Spirit that gives direction and builds strength, the Spirit that instills knowledge and Fear-of-GOD.
Isaiah 11:1–2 MSG

Anticipation

That "Shoot" and "Branch" was Jesus—an age-old hope finally sprung to life in a newborn Child. But He didn't come alone; in fact, He was never alone except for one moment on the cross when the Father turned away. No, Jesus experienced an unending fellowship and partnership with the Holy Spirit and the Father. Together, the three of them—which we call the Trinity—pulled off the biggest rescue in history.

The Holy Spirit brought powerful resources to Jesus' earthly ministry: wisdom, understanding, direction, strength, knowledge, and the fear of the Lord. And the Spirit will anoint you with the same empowering assets for your work in the Rebellion. You are not alone. Today, you are clothed in divine insight and understanding; you have the strength and guidance to move boldly forward in God's purposes and witness God's results.

Fill me afresh this day, God. I give You my attention and look for Your every resource to accomplish Your will today.

Jesus was going all over Galilee, teaching in their synagogues, preaching the good news of the kingdom, and healing every disease and sickness among the people.
Matthew 4:23 HCSB

day 353

Activation

Jesus waited a long time and lived many years before being initiated into active ministry. Yet He was never frantic or driven in His work; instead, He valued the preparations in body, soul, and spirit that God led Him through before releasing Him into three years of the supernatural. The servant is not greater than His master, right? So you, too, can expect seasons of preparation where it doesn't appear that much is going on through your gifts. Can you embrace those times?

But then there comes the time when you are activated. God begins to open up doors of opportunity beyond what you would have imagined or even chosen. Then it's time to move boldly into doing what Jesus did: Tell the good news of your story. Heal the sick. Lead people to a radical encounter with Jesus!

God, I embrace Your mission. Whether I'm in preparation mode or in activation mode, I affirm my part in Your world-changing ministry.

day 354

Jesus uttered another loud cry and breathed his last. And the curtain in the Temple was torn in two, from top to bottom. When the Roman officer who stood facing him saw how he had died, he exclaimed, "Truly, this was the Son of God!"
Mark 15:37–39 NLT

Revelation

Satan thought he had won. But even in death Jesus was powerfully active, drawing people into the Rebellion against sin and separation. This was potently evidenced in the tearing of the Temple curtain.

This curtain separated the Holy Place where the priests served from the Most Holy Place where God's glory resided. The presence of God was unapproachable except once a year for the high priest; it was sectioned off by a heavy curtain. But at the moment of Christ's death, this curtain was supernaturally torn in half, top to bottom.

Suddenly, there was no longer any separation! The message was that women and men can now draw near to God without the need of a human priest. Jesus is your High Priest, and He has permanently opened the door of access. You follow Jesus in drawing people into the Presence.

God, let my life be a powerful invitation for people to come close to You and find reconciliation. Let me live out Your presence today.

day
355

I tell you the truth. It is to your advantage that I go away; for if I do not go away, the Helper will not come to you; but if I depart, I will send Him to you.
John 16:7 NKJV

Multiplication

Not only was Jesus filled, strengthened, and guided by the Spirit; He sent the Spirit to do the same for all His disciples, exploding His impact upon planet Earth even as He departed earth. While Jesus was here, the Spirit would come upon people at certain times for certain tasks, but at Pentecost, the Spirit came to take up residence inside the followers of Jesus.

No one wanted to see Jesus leave, but afterward they recognized the genius of His plan. The Twelve became the seventy; the seventy became the five hundred; the five hundred became three thousand. And so multiplied the church of Jesus Christ until today, when millions bear the name and authority of Jesus through the New Rebellion. Are you experiencing the help of the Helper? Are you leading others to be filled with the Spirit too?

Holy Spirit of God, I want to be helped, counseled, and comforted by You! I want Your wisdom and boldness to lead me into Your will.

day
356

In My Father's house are many dwelling places; if it were not so, I would have told you; for I go to prepare a place for you.
John 14:2 NASB

Preparation

Jesus' destiny led Him from heaven to earth to live out the Kingdom life, defeat the power of sin, and initiate a Rebellion. Finally, He returned to heaven to prepare for the final gathering of all God's children into their eternal joy, into the community you were ultimately made for. He's not resting on His laurels; He continues to direct the Rebellion from headquarters in heaven.

And once again, your role follows His. You are serving His plan of preparation by bringing the culture of the Kingdom into your life and into your world as widely and deeply as possible. The more you become like Christ, the more prepared you are to live with Him forever. The more your life in Christ allures others to the beauty of heaven, the more you help them prepare for the future.

I determine to live intentionally, God. My life will be one of preparation and purpose, bringing a heavenly fragrance into the stuff of earth.

"I, Jesus, have sent my angel to give you this testimony for the churches. I am the Root and the Offspring of David, and the bright Morning Star." The Spirit and the bride say, "Come!" . . . Whoever is thirsty, let him come; and whoever wishes, let him take the free gift of the water of life.

Revelation 22:16–17 NIV

The War Ends

Revelation, the final book in the Bible, describes how the New Rebellion is finally won. Spiritual war, that began with Satan's thwarted coup attempt, that spoiled the paradise of Eden, whose tide was turned upon the cross, will finally be concluded. Those who serve the Rebellion will lay down their weapons and be united into a lasting heavenly peace. Satan and his demons will receive the judgment they've earned. A new heaven and a new earth will be in the making, and life will be good.

Until that glorious day, the message of the Rebellion is "Come!" The day of salvation is here: If you're thirsty, come to the source of living water and drink! Human history is the story of Jesus reaching and calling for the thirsty, and for your brief time upon life's stage, you echo that redemptive call!

God, I can't wait for that glorious day of renewal! But in the meantime, I'm Yours to amplify Your call of life to the thirsty.

day 358

If you cling to your life, you will lose it;
but if you give it up for me, you will find it.
Matthew 10:39 NLT

Lost and Found

As the leader of the New Rebellion, Jesus packs many surprises. When you expect Him to be harsh, He is extraordinarily gentle. And just when you get used to Jesus' gentleness, He challenges you with impossible tasks. In the immortal words of C. S. Lewis, "He is not a tame lion."

Every person has an instinctive grip upon their own wellbeing. Yet Jesus requires you to let it go, with no guarantee other than your trust in His character. Make no mistake: This is scary stuff! You no longer have the final choice of where you will live, who you will marry, what your occupation will be, and who your friends are. Everything you hold dear must be given to Him to do with as He pleases. And what He pleases will not always please you! But it will be very, very good!

God, I'm not looking for any safety nets, any Plan B's. I'm ready to lose it all into Your hands, and I know I'll be found.

"If you want to give it all you've got," Jesus replied, "go sell your possessions; give everything to the poor. All your wealth will then be in heaven. Then come follow me."
Matthew 19:21 MSG

day 359

No Clenched Fists

God has a way of knowing exactly the thing you most crave in life, the thing above all others that you desire—respect, position, pleasure, a dream perhaps, a person, or an accomplishment. Whatever it is, sooner or later, Jesus will give you the opportunity to give it up, either the thing itself or the drive to obtain it.

See, I knew it! Jesus just wants to take all the good stuff away from me! Not so.

Jesus knows that what you grasp white-knuckled in fact grasps you. He knows that if no earthly thing possesses you, then you will be free from the dominion of earth. Your rebellion against the Deceiver will be effective, and you'll find your heart's desires fully satisfied in the gifts of God. This is a crucial test of the Kingdom of God—will you pass?

God, there is no one else who requires as much as You—and no other to whom I could ever trust to give up my everything.

day 360

I say to you, do not resist an evil person; but whoever slaps you on your right cheek, turn the other to him also.
Matthew 5:39 NASB

The End of the Story

Every good story has a bad guy. The movies you love almost always have some form of villain, don't they? And no matter how evil they are in the beginning, there's nothing like seeing them brought to justice in the end. Why is this the classic tale? Because it's the story you live within. There is a war; there is a good Guy and a bad guy. And, in the end, the villain will get what's coming to him!

Which is why it's not up to you to enforce personal justice now. This is a distinctive of the Rebellion. The world frequently neglects governmental justice, yet tries to enforce personal justice; but they've got it backward. Jesus calls rulers and governments to a high standard of justice—that is their job. But on the personal level, His call is to overcome evil with good.

God, I trust that You will bring justice to this world, and in the meantime, I receive Your grace to return good for evil.

Whoever causes the downfall of one of these little ones who believe in Me—it would be better for him if a heavy millstone were hung around his neck and he were thrown into the sea.
Mark 9:42 HCSB

day 361

No Swimming Allowed!

These are some more strong words from Jesus! And since Jesus is more about saving people than drowning them, this points to the fact that Jesus has very strong feelings about this topic. It's also a foreshadowing of the day of justice to come.

His ire is loosed upon those who lead young people astray, particularly those who believe in Jesus as a child or teenager and yet are influenced by older, stronger folks to abandon their faith. Maybe it's a drug-dealer that lures the naive into destruction. Maybe it's a college professor that systematically undermines a supernatural worldview among his or her students. Whoever it is, they will pay the ultimate penalty for their spiritual assassinations. The mission of the Rebellion is the converse: to rescue those whose faith is weak and give them something to believe in again.

Help me, God, to be very careful how I treat young people—in word and deed, I want to point them to the awesomeness of You!

day 362

Why do you look at the speck in your brother's eye, but do not consider the plank in your own eye?
Matthew 7:3 NKJV

Eyedrops, Anyone?

Jesus' words continue to challenge and confront those who would be Rebels with a cause. From childhood, you learn how to elevate yourself, theoretically, by tearing down someone else. Someone more vulnerable. It doesn't really bring personal elevation, of course, but it can produce a certain feeling of power. As adults, the pattern of criticizing others merely becomes more sophisticated or not.

But Jesus went to the root and declared that you have no business criticizing your brother or sister, especially when your own sin looms large. Judgment is not a Kingdom virtue; humility is what finds favor and advancement in the Rebellion. This motivation tends to be a real blind spot, and Jesus' solution is to spend your effort upon your own holiness more than others' failures. From that place, you can gently and kindly help your brother with his issues.

Give me Your eyes, God, to see myself authentically and others mercifully. Instill in me an enduring humility for Your honor and others' blessing.

You have heard that it was said to the people long ago, "Do not murder, and anyone who murders will be subject to judgment." But I tell you that anyone who is angry with his brother will be subject to judgment.
Matthew 5:21–22 NIV

Straight to the Heart

Jesus used the Sermon on the Mount to illuminate several Old Testament commandments. Essentially, He took exterior actions that were clearly immoral and then made an *internal* application. In other words, it's not enough to just keep yourself from doing evil actions, you have to guard against evil motivations in your heart! Jesus was highlighting the fact that bad actions flow from bad thinking, and the heart is where the real battles are won or lost.

Anger is a very powerful emotion. Anger trumpets that something inside you is out of alignment and needs to come into agreement with God. There *are* times when God is angry, and agreement with God includes your feeling "righteous" anger. But managing anger righteously is not something that humans do very well. In the New Rebellion, anger is an emotion best left to God.

Search my heart, O God. Keep me focused today, not just on right outward behavior, but on a heart condition that is fully in tune with You.

day 364

If you are kind only to your friends, how are you different from anyone else? Even pagans do that. But you are to be perfect, even as your Father in heaven is perfect.
Matthew 5:47–48 NLT

The Impossible Dream?

Perfection eludes the most brilliant and noble of souls. And yet perfection is what you are made for. Eden was a place of absolute agreement and fellowship with God; it was perfection. Heaven, too, will be a place where no imperfect attitude or action exists in any form. This is your destiny; this is who you really are!

On planet Earth, however, you wrestle against a very imperfect flesh, which tries to hinder your true self from coming forth. The Father's agenda is to continually purify your heart and bring you more and more into alignment with Himself: kindness to enemies, a servant heart, courage under fire, an unstoppable love—these are some of the passions of the Rebellion. This is the perfecting influence of the Holy Spirit that moves you closer every day to the impossible dream!

Teach me the heavenly skill of loving my enemies, God. Refine my heart today so that I can take my place effectively in the New Rebellion.

day 365

Work out your own salvation with fear and trembling.
Philippians 2:12 NKJV

Live on Purpose

When Paul lays out the challenge above, he is *not* admonishing you to "obtain" your salvation by your own effort. Rather, his urgent call is to "live out" your salvation with intentionality. In other words, don't be passive about activating your Kingdom life in the practical outworkings of today!

These are days for action that transcends intention. These are days to make every moment count! To live out the life you believe in every detail of your existence. If you value worship, then be a radical worshipper. If you value compassion, then practice it extravagantly. Let every activity you set your heart to be a reflection of your heavenly calling and heavenly destiny. Search out and eliminate every discrepancy between *who you want to be* and *who your are* . . . so that the beauty of Christ may dazzle the world as He expresses Himself through you.

Lord, You know I was born for a holy uprising!
Now transform me so that everything ordinary
in my life becomes extraordinary.

I want to make a difference, God. I want my life and my faith to have an impact upon the culture and society I live within.